**New Eastern Europe**

NEW EASTERN EUROPE IS A COLLABORATIVE PROJECT BETWEEN THREE POLISH PARTNERS

The City of Gdańsk
www.gdansk.pl

GDAŃSK
city of freedom

A city with over a thousand years of history, Gdańsk has been a melting pot of cultures and ethnic groups. The air of tolerance and wealth built on trade has enabled culture, science, and the Arts to flourish in the city for centuries. Today, Gdańsk remains a key meeting place and major tourist attraction in Poland. While the city boasts historic sites of enchanting beauty, it also has a major historic and social importance. In addition to its 1000-year history, the city is the place where the Second World War broke out as well as the birthplace of Solidarność, the Solidarity movement, which led to the fall of Communism in Central and Eastern Europe.

The European Solidarity Centre
www.ecs.gda.pl

 **ECS** european solidarity centre

The European Solidarity Centre is a multifunctional institution combining scientific, cultural and educational activities with a modern museum and archive, which documents freedom movements in the modern history of Poland and Europe.
The Centre was established in Gdańsk on November 8th 2007. Its new building was opened in 2014 on the anniversary of the August Accords signed in Gdańsk between the worker's union "Solidarność" and communist authorities in 1980. The Centre is meant to be an agora, a space for people and ideas that build and develop a civic society, a meeting place for people who hold the world's future dear. The mission of the Centre is to commemorate, maintain and popularise the heritage and message of the Solidarity movement and the anti-communist democratic opposition in Poland and throughout the world. Through its activities the Centre wants to inspire new cultural, civic, trade union, local government, national and European initiatives with a universal dimension.

The Jan Nowak-Jeziorański College of Eastern Europe
www.kew.org.pl

The Jan Nowak-Jeziorański
College of Eastern Europe in Wrocław

The College of Eastern Europe is a non-profit, non-governmental foundation founded on February 9th 2001 by Jan Nowak-Jeziorański, a former head of the Polish section of Radio Free Europe and a democratic activist. The foundation deals with cooperation between the nations of Central and Eastern Europe. The aims if its charters are to carry out educational, cultural and publishing activities, and to develop programmes which enhance the transformation in the countries of Eastern Europe. The organisation has its headquarters in Wrocław, Poland, a city in western Poland, perfectly situated in the centre of Europe and with a deep understanding of both Western and Eastern Europe.

Dear Reader,

Do many people think of political prisoners in Europe today? Or have politicians in countries that still uphold this despicable practice managed to deflect western criticism in exchange for business transactions and promises of stability? In rocky times, the latter is especially tempting.

No matter what the exchange deal is, it is clear that silencing dissent and oppressing individuals based on political views is something we cannot ignore. That is why this issue of *New Eastern Europe* aims to show the plight of the political prisoners whose voices we barely hear. Our contributors include former prisoners themselves, Andrei Sannikov and Rasul Jafarov, as well as other authors who illustrate the alarming increase in oppressions in the post-Soviet space. Reading them should help us understand the dire situation of today's freedom fighters and encourage greater solidarity towards their cause. As Sannikov writes, "political prisoners are jailed for their beliefs and principles. They fight for freedom, not just of their countries, but for all of us."

Continued attention also needs to be paid to Ukraine, where changes are being implemented even if some elements of the landscape remain the same. Yulia Tymoshenko is hungry for power again and appears willing to do whatever it takes to make a comeback. Our author, Ukrainian journalist Roman Romanyuk, explains why Tymoshenko's ratings are on the rise. As the situation with Crimea becomes more tense, the position of its Tatar population is only getting worse. It is presented in Igor Semyvolos's text. Finally, while the western media talk about the possibility of war in Ukraine's eastern parts, our reporters, Paweł Pieniążek and Wojciech Koźmic, show that in the two self-proclaimed republics, the war has never stopped.

We close this issue with a special section on Kraków and Lviv – two UNESCO Cities of Literature. Our authors here highlight the numerous connections between these two cultural capitals and the flourishing literary life that characterises them today. We invite you to taste them yourself.

As always we welcome your feedback. Contact us at editors@neweasterneurope.eu and stay in touch with us online at www.neweasterneurope.eu as well as via Facebook and Twitter.

The Editors

Contents

www.neweasterneurope.eu

EDITOR AND PUBLISHER
The Jan Nowak-Jeziorański College
of Eastern Europe in Wrocław
office@kew.org.pl, www.kew.org.pl

Zamek Wojnowice
ul. Zamkowa 2, 55-330 Wojnowice, Poland

CO-EDITOR
European Solidarity Centre
ecs@ecs.gda.pl, www.ecs.gda.pl

EDITORIAL BOARD
Leonidas Donskis, Yaroslav Hrytsak,
Paweł Kowal, Ivan Krastev, Georges Mink,
Zdzisław Najder, Cornelius Ochmann,
Mykola Riabchuk, Eugeniusz Smolar,
Lilia Shevtsova, Roman Szporluk, Jan Zielonka

EDITORIAL TEAM
Adam Reichardt, Editor-in-Chief
Iwona Reichardt, Deputy Editor, Lead Translator
Agnieszka Pikulicka-Wilczewska, Editor
Igor Lyubashenko, Contributing Editor
Stuart Feltis, Editorial Intern
Zofia Fenikowska, Editorial Researcher

COPYEDITING
Jan Ryland

ILLUSTRATIONS AND COVER
Andrzej Zaręba

COVER LAYOUT
Do Lasu s.c

SUBSCRIPTION
dystrybucja@kew.org.pl

LAYOUT AND FORMATTING
Małgorzata Chyc | AT Wydawnictwo

EDITORIAL OFFICES
New Eastern Europe
ul. Mazowiecka 25 p. 808, 30-019 Kraków
editors@neweasterneurope.eu

European Solidarity Centre
Plac Solidarności 1, 80-863 Gdańsk
tel.: +48 58 767 79 71
ecs@ecs.gda.pl

New Eastern Europe is funded in part by a grant from
the Taube Foundation for Jewish Life and Culture

New Eastern Europe is co-financed by the
Polish Ministry of Culture and National Heritage.

**Ministry of
Culture
and National
Heritage of
the Republic
of Poland.**

The special section on Kraków and Lviv as cities
of literature is co-financed by the City of Kraków.

Legal Services Provided by KOKSZTYS S.A.

KOKSZTYS

Circulation: 5000
Printing: Zakład Graficzny "Colonel" S.A.
International Distribution: www.pineapple-media.com
Printed in Poland

Existence without life

ANDREI SANNIKOV

One thing that has to be remembered about political prisoners is that their fate directly and proportionally depends on support inside a country, international attention, solidarity and action. For political prisoners, it is extremely important to know that they are not forgotten and that their sacrifice is being recognised, both in their countries and around the world.

On December 8th 1986 at 23:50, in the hospital of a watch factory in the town of Chistopol, Tatar Autonomous Soviet Socialist Republic, Anatoly Marchenko, a Soviet prisoner of conscience, died at the age of 48. He was transferred to this hospital from prison after his health deteriorated dramatically as a result of a hunger strike that he declared in August of the same year and continued for several months. He wrote in his letter, which was published 12 years after his death: "Since August 4th I have been on a hunger strike, demanding a stop to the torture of political prisoners in the Soviet Union and their release." He was buried unnamed under number 646.

Five days after Marchenko's tragic death, Mikhail Gorbachev, the Secretary General of the Communist Party of the Soviet Union, ended the political exile of Andrei Sakharov and soon after all Soviet political prisoners were released. That ended the history of political imprisonment in the Soviet Union which was followed by the end of the state itself. Through his tragic death, Marchenko heralded an era of freedom on the territory of the former Soviet Union.

Strange and tragic

However, that freedom was very short-lived. After the collapse of the Soviet Union 25 years ago, the regimes of the former Soviet republics, now independent states, soon reverted to the repressive practices of the past. Over the years, these practices were perfected and became some of the most effective tools used by autocratic and dictatorial regimes in order to maintain their power indefinitely.

> After the collapse of the Soviet Union, the regimes in the former Soviet republics quickly reverted to the repressive practices of the past, which became effective tools for the regimes to maintain their power indefinitely.

In Belarus events were developing in a very strange and tragic way. In the beginning, of all the former Soviet republics, Belarus was the only parliamentary state. Moreover, it was at the forefront of establishing an internationally recognised democracy. It was the first post-Soviet state to apply for membership in the Council of Europe, as it was understood that this was a necessary step to being recognised as a democracy (today, it is the only European state that is not a member of the Council). Belarus was also one of the first to recognise and adopt the Optional Protocol to the International Covenant on Political and Civil Rights, a taboo in the Soviet Union since it empowered individuals to defend human rights against their own state. During this short period of liberalisation and recognition of international standards in the area of human rights protection, Belarus made a huge contribution to international security in both nuclear and conventional terms. It is yet further proof that only a democratic country can be a real contributor to security, regardless of whether it is based on hard or soft power.

The dangers posed by power-hungry Alyaksandr Lukashenka, who became the first president of Belarus, were underestimated, both inside the country and internationally. He ushered in a new era of ruthless, greedy, internationally irresponsible and unpredictable rulers in the three founding members of the Commonwealth of Independent States, a divorce mechanism established to avoid bloodshed on the territory of the former Soviet Union. The leaders of Belarus, Russia and Ukraine, Stanislav Shushkevich, Boris Yeltsin and Leonid Kravchuk, who dissolved the totalitarian state were long gone from power and their successors were busy reversing the process of democratisation in the former Soviet republics. One exception has been Ukraine, which made a second and more serious attempt to break away from the past and stop the authoritarian tendencies in its politics. It is now trying to build its democratic and independent future.

In Belarus Lukashenka has managed to build a model of a dictatorial state that is quite eagerly and effectively exploited by Vladimir Putin. The same model is also utilised in other former Soviet states and was brought to its logical, aggressive completion by the Kremlin, which started war in Europe against Ukraine. The uncertainty of the 1990s transformed into the consolidation of autocratic and dictatorial regimes that created a true "cooperative of dictators", consisting of a majority of the former Soviet republics. Their leaders may be at odds with each other on different issues such as economic, social, trade and even political matters, but they always agree and support each other's contempt for human rights and basic freedoms.

The primary shared attribute of all these regimes is political prisoners, people who are thrown in jail for their political beliefs that do not coincide with the views of a ruling group and who are not afraid to speak up and act publicly against the regimes in their respective countries. It is quite indicative that Belarus was not known for any serious human rights violations in the first few years following the collapse of the Soviet Union. It all started when Lukashenka came to power and since then, the situation has only been getting worse.

Vulnerabilities

One thing should be remembered about political prisoners and political repression in general: it illustrates both the nature and the vulnerabilities of a regime. Repression is directed at the parties a regime considers to be its greatest threat(s). This can even take the form of political assassination, as was the case in Belarus where, in 1999, several opposition leaders were abducted and never seen again, notably Viktar Hanchar and Yuri Zaharenka. In Russia, several opposition politicians have been murdered, including most recently, Boris Nemtsov.

Nevertheless, dictatorial regimes are vulnerable, despite all their demonstrative strength. Firstly, they are not protected by international law. This is the most important factor in both domestic and international fight for freedom and against tyranny. Even though it looks as though dictators are happy to demonstrate their contempt for the international community, especially when it voices concerns or demands respect for human rights, they are in fact closely watching the international reaction to abuses and respond with harsher repressions when the reaction is weak.

It is interesting to note one striking phenomenon. Over the last 10–15 years, there has been a visible increase in the number of human rights organisations, both domestic and international. At the same time, there has been a marked growth in both the number and severity of human rights violations. This is not because of the failure of human right defenders, the majority of whom are committed, courageous and honest. Rather, the failure of the relevant intergovernmental organisations to uphold human rights standards is to blame. In Europe, where Belarus belongs, the relevant organisations include the Council of Europe, the European Union and the Organisation for Security and Co-operation in Europe (OSCE). Their failure to act directly affects the human rights situation in countries like Belarus.

Unfortunately, there is an increasing tendency towards realpolitik practices regarding human rights issues. This tendency was strengthened following the invasion of Ukraine by Russia and pro-Russian forces. European and international organisations that are founded on strong democratic principles have begun diluting these foundations by taking soft positions on human rights abuses, justifying them by referring to "changed geopolitical circumstances". They increasingly yield to the pressure of dictatorial regimes and their supporters. Geopolitical, economic, and business arguments have begun to prevail in many cases where dictatorial regimes, such as Belarus, are discussed and decisions are made. As a result, human rights have fallen victim to the politics of "new pragmatism".

> In these times of multiple European and global crises, the need to uphold values has become pressing.

This is especially true of the parliamentary bodies in those institutions which tend to overlook human rights abuses and tacitly support repressive governments and pro-government NGOs. There is a tendency to choose or even help create think-tanks that are closely linked to the regimes and base an overall assessment of the situation on their loyal analyses. It has to be stressed that such policies have never been successful and that more often than not, they lead to harsher repressions by a regime, provoke disturbances inside a dictatorship and destabilise the situation in a region. In this time of multiple European and global crises, the need to uphold values has become pressing. The values matter. Placing emphasis on them helps solve geopolitical problems, not vice versa.

International support

It is important to remember that the fate of political prisoners directly and proportionally depends on international attention, solidarity and action. Of course, the key element is domestic solidarity and attention, which in turn leads to international campaigns. When we speak of political prisoners, we refer to non-democratic countries that have no separation of powers and no independent judicial system. In these cases, the international community can act as a democratic judiciary, highlighting human rights violations and demanding an end to them. The absence of international pressure leads to more impunity for the perpetrators, both individual officials and state institutions.

For political prisoners, it is extremely important to know that they are not forgotten and that their sacrifice is being recognised, both in their countries and around the world. I understand this very well based on my own experience, when I was thrown behind bars for running against "the last dictator in Europe" and recognised by the international community as a political prisoner.

There are two kinds of approaches to being in prison. Some argue that in prison, there is life and even freedom: it just depends on the person and his or her perception of reality. Others disagree.

I belong to the latter camp. For me, prison is existence without life. Moreover, I believe that it is dangerous to presume any normality in an abnormal situation when one is deprived of freedom. It is an ordeal that

> It often happens that attention is focused on better known names, while lesser known individuals are ignored. Tyrannies understand this and apply their repressive practices accordingly.

one has to go through in the fight for freedom and principles and try to survive. However, behind bars, it is crucial to have a strong connection with the outside world, because it is outside prison that life and freedom exist. That is why letters of support to political prisoners are so important. Receiving support from people who you do not know is as important as the backing and love of family and friends.

Political prisoners are jailed for their beliefs and principles. They fight for freedom, not just of their countries, but for all of us. They care about freedom and justice, they care about us and that is why we must care about them. Speaking of international attention to the plight of political prisoners, it is important to remember that we cannot create "first class" and "second class" prisoners. It is often the case that attention is focused on better known names, while lesser known individuals are ignored. Tyrannies understand this and apply their repressive practices accordingly. Their purpose is to make repressions invisible to the outside world and ensure they are ignored by the international community. By harassing and jailing less visible activists, they try to achieve two goals simultaneously: to keep society under control and under pressure and to avoid the strong international reaction that would inevitably ensue if more prominent activists are incarcerated.

This is what is currently happening in Belarus, where the regime, under the burden of international pressure, released some well-known political prisoners to placate public opinion but then immediately began to jail other, less "famous" hostages, such as human rights defender Mikhail Zhemchuzhny. European politicians who are eager to improve relations with Lukashenka prefer to ignore these facts, consequently easing pressure on the regime to change. This kind of "new pragmatism" will only lead to new and harsher repressions.

Not long ago in Łódź, I had the opportunity to listen to the famous Chinese dissident, author, musician and poet Liao Yiwu, who spent several years in a communist prison. He impressed me with one very simple thought: "The Berlin Wall would not have fallen if not for the Tiananmen Square protests." He said in very simple terms that the fight for freedom is universal and has to be supported by the democratic world, in every corner of the world.

Anatoly Marchenko's tragic sacrifice led to the freedom of many because of the strong reaction it provoked around the world. The attention and reaction of ordinary people, the media, human rights defenders and all those who care about any political prisoner is of great importance, since it really does force politicians to act. That is the power of those who care and that power can make our world a better place. NEE⟩

Andrei Sannikov is a Belarusian activist and politician who ran in the 2010 presidential elections and was later imprisoned for his political protest (2010–2012).

A new generation of Russian political prisoners

JANEK LASOCKI

Russians who are currently behind bars for political reasons are a good representation of the country that Vladimir Putin's Russia has become. They are being punished for exercising their fundamental freedoms, for exposing the web of corruption on which the state is built and for threatening local oligarchs loyal to the Kremlin. Often, they are imprisoned for all three.

33-year old Ildar Dadin is a former security guard who got married in a Moscow detention centre last February. Cameras were not allowed for the short ceremony but journalist Anastasiya Zotova, now his wife, came out smiling to the well-wishers and reporters waiting in the snow. At that point, Dadin had been under house arrest or behind bars for a year, having neither had any previous convictions nor a particularly high pubic profile. The judge at Moscow's Basmanny Court had sentenced Dadin to a total of three years of prison.

Anastasiya wrote on her blog about Dadin and the conditions he faced. Determined to stay in high spirits, he had been studying law textbooks he managed to obtain (with the hope of one day finishing a law degree) but it has not been easy. In one of the other detention centres he stayed in, he joined other inmates in catching mice with empty milk cartons in order to pass the time.

His crime had been holding demonstrations in small groups or on his own, repeatedly and without permission. He organised and held a one-man picket in support of the peaceful protestors in the "Bolotnoe Delo", a three man protest against Russian military involvement in Ukraine, and, on a separate occasion, in support of oppositionist Alexei Navalny. After each of these little acts was noticed, he was either fined up to 15,000 roubles or served 15 days in prison. When the authorities decided to combine these acts, he was found to be violating a new law restricting peaceful assembly. He was punished for exercising a fundamental right in Russia's own constitution. Today, Dadin is part of a new generation of political prisoners in Vladimir Putin's Russia, punished for their beliefs and for having the courage to express them. The Russian human rights organisation Memorial maintains a list of those it considers political prisoners and at last count, the number had reached 87. Alarmingly, it is rising.

Gradual deterioration

Recent Russian history is no stranger to political prisoners. The Soviet era dissidents Sergey Kovalev, Andrei Sakharov and Alexander Solzhenitsyn are just some of the better known prisoners among the thousands who were imprisoned in the Soviet Union for their political or religious beliefs. In Tsarist times, many of the first inhabitants of Siberia were critical writers or political dissenters who had drawn the ire of the Tsar and been sent into exile. However, post-Cold War Russia was supposed to be different. A signatory to the European Convention of Human Rights, Russia adopted the rhetoric of the West when it came to that issue. After the fall of the Soviet Union, civil society blossomed and independent media outlets multiplied.

After Vladimir Putin first took his seat in the Kremlin, the sanctity of fundamental freedoms gradually deteriorated and efforts were made to once again rewrite history. Even so, a few high profile cases aside (such as that of Mikhail Khodorkovsky), the situation ten years ago was not as bad as it is today. Demonstrators would face small fines or 15 days behind bars, but little more. The "white ribbon" demonstrations that rocked Moscow after the 2011 parliamentary elections changed everything. Legislation was passed against peaceful demonstrations and criticism of the government. State media began broadcasting even more aggressive propaganda (particularly after the events in Ukraine) and the number of political prisoners dramatically increased.

Although the Memorial Human Rights Centre keeps the authoritative list, there is no universally agreed upon definition of a political prisoner in Russia. The Moscow-based SOVA Centre for Information and Analysis publishes lists of those who are unjustifiably behind bars for so-called "crimes of an extremist nature"; Amnesty International prefers the term "prisoner of conscience" and uses it sparingly, while a number of far-right nationalist groups have called jailed members of their organisations political prisoners. However, Memorial bases its decisions on who to define as a political prisoner according to a 2012 resolution by the Council of Europe Parliamentary Assembly (PACE). This includes those prosecuted exclusively in connection with belonging to an ethnic, religious or other group or for convictions or views. They also include those who have prosecuted selectively or sentenced disproportionately when a case is politically motivated.

Those Russians who are currently behind bars are a good representation of the country that Putin's Russia has become. They are being punished for exercising their fundamental freedoms, including any political opposition, for exposing the web of corruption on which the state is built and for threatening local barons loyal to the Kremlin. Often, they are imprisoned for all three.

Ukrainian hostages

However, it is symbolic that the best known political prisoners over the past couple of years are Ukrainian. Since the end of the EuroMaidan demonstrations in Kyiv and the onset of the Ukraine-Russia conflict, at least 30 Ukrainian nationals have been detained (often subject to torture) and imprisoned on charges including terrorism, murder and espionage. The most famous among them was the fiery Nadiya Savchenko, who was captured in Donbas and transferred to Rostov where she endured a farcical trial, including being accused of complicity in the murder of Russian journalists. As a result of a prisoner exchange, she was returned to Kyiv amid much fanfare in May 2016. This was in no small part thanks to international support and the success of the "Let my people go" campaign.

> Since the end of the EuroMaidan demonstrations in Kyiv and the onset of the Ukraine-Russia conflict, at least 30 Ukrainian nationals have been detained in Russia.

Even so, many remain behind bars, including Ukrainian businessmen accused of espionage and others accused of genocide or participation in the first Chechen War. There are also a large number of prisoners from Crimea, including Oleksandr Kolchenko, Oleg Sentsov and many Crimean Tartars who have been given astonishingly long sentences. As Amnesty International wrote recently, this whole process "played into Russia's propaganda war against Ukraine and was redolent of Stalinist-era show trials".

Russians themselves have faced a curtailing of their basic rights, with the freedom of assembly being heavily restricted. The most famous case, the so-called "Bolotnoye Delo", involved 30 participants in the peaceful post-election marches of 2011–12 that were violently broken up by police. Denis Lutskevich was 20 years

Photo: S0157538 (CC)commons.wikimedia.org

In Russia the freedom of assembly is being heavily restricted. The most famous case is the "Bolotnoye Delo" protest which was violently broken up by police and led to the arrest of nearly 30 people. In the photo a protestor holds a sign that says "The Bolotnaya square case is a fiction" outside the courthouse during one of the trials.

old and finishing his first year at university when he was detained and ultimately sentenced to three and a half years in prison. "After my arrest, I thought that surely I would be released soon. I was not guilty; I believed it must be a misunderstanding and that they would find me innocent. Yet they did not let me go... it was very frightening."

Lutskevich spent two years in a detention centre, in a small, stuffy cell with up to ten other inmates before finally being released. He is now trying to rebuild his life. Four years after the demonstrations, arrests continue to be made. In April 2016 Maksim Panfilov became the latest person to be taken into custody.

Expressing one's views online, in print or creatively, is now more dangerous than ever. Rafis Kashapov, a Tatar activist from Tatarstan, was charged in 2015 with extremism and inciting ethnic hatred after condemning the annexation of Crimea on social media. Similarly, Andrei Bubayev, a 40-year old electrician from Tver, was sentenced to two years for sharing an article critical of Crimea's annexation and a photo of a tube of toothpaste with the caption "Squeeze Russia out of yourself". Vladimir Podrezov was jailed for taking part in a stunt to paint a Soviet star on top of a Russian skyscraper with Ukrainian national colours.

Keeping up appearances

Opposition politicians, though generally very weak, are targeted if they are considered to be a threat or suddenly gain a lot of support. Oleg Navalny, the brother of anti-corruption activist and oppositionist Alexei, was sentenced to three years for embezzlement in a case which Memorial claimed was really about stopping "Alexei's public activity and the threats his activities create for the current government". Similarly, Andrei Pivovarov was a campaign manager in the only region where the opposition was allowed to compete in the 2015 local elections and found himself charged with bribery.

Those who uncover local corruption or question a regional oligarch's propaganda are also punished. Evgeny Vitishko, an environmental campaigner who investigated damage caused by the Sochi Winter Olympics, was imprisoned after looking into the unlawful seizure of land by the governor of Krasnodar. Sergei Nikiforov was found guilty of bribery after leading protests against a gold mining company in the Far East region of Amur. While in Chechnya, the police framed Ruslan Kutaev, "finding" drugs in his home which lead to a four-year sentence. He was targeted because of his efforts to highlight the tragic history of Stalin's deportations of the Chechens, an event that Ramzan Kadyrov, the head of the Chechen Republic, has tried to downplay.

For all its increasing restrictions on personal freedoms, the Kremlin is keen on maintaining the appearance of a developed country with democratic legitimacy. There are three things that are enabling Russia to maintain this facade: control of the courts, a growing amount of legislation that can be used to justify its actions and the people the state is choosing to put behind bars.

Sergey Smirnov is chief editor of the online portal *Media Zona*, which monitors the judicial and prison system in Russia. As he explains, "For a long time, Russia has lacked independent courts. The justice system today has a clear chain of command. The head of a regional court has total control over his judges and he makes no decisions himself without consulting his superiors. It is the same at every level. In politically-motivated cases, this is especially noticeable: sentences are passed in agreement with the Kremlin." Hard evidence of this is difficult to come by, although in February 2011, following Mikhail Khodorkovsky's second show trial, Natalia Vasilyeva, an assistant to Viktor Danilkin, the judge in the case, gave an interview to *Gazeta*.

> For all its increasing restrictions on personal freedoms, the Kremlin is keen on maintaining the appearance of a modern country with democratic legitimacy.

ru describing how Danilkin had to consult with the higher-ranking Moscow City Court throughout the entire trial. She claimed that ultimately, he had the verdict imposed on him from above, after his first draft was rejected.

Today, Russian courts are able to use a wide array of new criminal legislation that, although unconstitutional in the way it restricts basic rights, has armed judges with the legal means to imprison anyone the Kremlin deems a threat. For example, Article 212.1 of the Russian Criminal Code (multiple violations of the established order of organising or holding gatherings, demonstrations and pickets) was used to charge Ildar Dadin. Article 280.1 (which broaches public calls to violate the territorial integrity of the Russian Federation) was introduced to punish anyone criticising the annexation of Crimea. The broad description and interpretation of the definition of "extremism" has also given a lot of space to silence activists such as Vadim Tyumentsev, a video blogger from Tomsk who was sentenced to five years after calling on people to attend a protest against high transport fares and for criticising the Russian intervention in Ukraine.

High price

The Kremlin has also been careful about who it chooses to put behind bars. Unlike Egypt, which jailed thousands of government opponents, or Azerbaijan, where political prisoners have included the most prominent human rights lawyers, investigative journalists and political activists, by and large, the Kremlin seems to have intentionally targeted individuals or small groups with a low profile. These are people without networks in the West and who are not household names, even among the liberal opposition-supporting minority. The better-known leaders of civil society are instead hit with hefty fines, their work is obstructed and their reputation attacked on state TV. Meanwhile, Russians across the country are getting the message that life is possible, but expressing any sort of opposition risks a high price.

> The Kremlin seems to have intentionally targeted individuals or small groups with a low profile. These are people without networks in the West and who are not household names.

Any real change of direction towards openness and judicial reform is now unimaginable under Putin. Indeed, the growing trend of locking opponents away is directly linked to how threatened those in the Kremlin feel; this has been compounded with sanctions and lower oil prices, making the economy less stable than it has been for years. In many areas, wages are being delayed and the number of strikes and protests is increasing.

Naturally, this will only continue to unnerve the government. The best that can be hoped for is that it does not get any worse, although under current circumstances, it is hard to be optimistic.

Ultimately, beyond the manipulation and politics are ordinary people, whose lives have been shattered. Most of them never imagined they would have to give up so much for expressing themselves peacefully, a right that is guaranteed in the Russian Federation's constitution. Organisations like Memorial and Open Russia have been able to provide them and their families with some help, and information about their plight is spread in the independent media. Yet outside of Russia, even less is known about this new generation of political prisoners. International pressure and attention can achieve small victories, as was demonstrated with some of the Ukrainians who were released. Therefore, if we ever want Russia to change, it is important that we do not neglect them. NEE)

Janek Lasocki is a senior programme officer for Europe and Central Asia with Article 19, an international human rights NGO.

Azerbaijan's very own Ivan Denisovichs

ARZU GEYBULLAYEVA

Azerbaijan is known for its poor record on human rights and the detention of its political prisoners. Yet, the regime continues to deny the existence of these prisoners while the West turns a blind eye to the abuses in the name of strategic partnership and energy co-operation. What more will it take to end the business-as-usual approach towards Azerbaijan?

In the letters he wrote while serving in the Red Army, Aleksandr Solzhenitsyn described Joseph Stalin in derogatory terms, calling him a *khozayin* (owner). This cost Solzhenitsyn his freedom. He was arrested, accused of anti-Soviet propaganda and establishing a hostile organisation. He was then sentenced to eight years in a labour camp. This experience was later described in detail in one of Solzhenitsyn's books titled *One day in the life of Ivan Denisovich*. In the book, the main character, Denisovich, was sentenced to ten years despite being innocent. For those familiar with Azerbaijan's repressive climate, there are many Ivan Denisovichs there. Moreover, their experiences differ little, if at all, from the treatment of dissidents in Solzhenitsyn's time.

"You know, together we have read it all – [Aleksandr] Solzhenitsyn, Varlaam Shalamov, [Vasily] Grossman, and [Vasily] Aksyonov. Together, we often discussed how spouses who had been arrested felt. In 1937, there were a great many of them. We just never would have predicted that the 21st century would have brought about the same levels of repression as the 1930s," Leyla Yunus, a political activist and human rights defender who was arrested in the summer of 2014, wrote to her husband, political scientist Arif Yunus, who was arrested just days after his wife.

After more than a year of custody, the couple were released as a result of Leyla Yunus's deteriorating health. She is currently undergoing medical treatment in the Netherlands.

Closed chapter

In her letter to Arif, Leyla wrote that the only difference between their story and that of the Soviet dissidents, like Solzhenitsyn, was age: "Solzhenitsyn was only 27 at the time of his arrest, while we are in our 60s," she wrote.

In the meantime, the government in Azerbaijan has refused to admit that there are any political prisoners in the country. President Ilham Aliyev and his closest allies within the cabinet have continuously dismissed critical claims that the country mistreats its outspoken men and women. These prisoners are simply referred to as criminals since they are in prison for offences such as tax evasion, embezzlement, illegal entrepreneurship, hooliganism, drug possession and abuse of power.

> The government in Azerbaijan has refused to admit there are any political prisoners in the country.

The authorities' confidence is not surprising. It is best illustrated by an event that occurred in 2013 when Aliyev, standing next to the then European Commission President José Manuel Barroso, buoyed by a resolution that rejected a report on political prisoners in Azerbaijan, ostentatiously said, "there are no political prisoners in Azerbaijan ... that chapter is closed." That critical resolution gave Aliyev the green light for what was later described by many international observers as an unprecedented crackdown. Shortly after the resolution, the Azerbaijani leadership embarked on a mission to silence its critics, the so-called criminals, who happened to be from various civil society platforms, political movements, youth groups and also included journalists and human rights defenders. Those who did not end up behind bars chose to tone down their criticism or leave the country altogether. As Eurasianet reported in 2015: "Azerbaijani applications for asylum in the European Union increased by 16 per cent between 2012, when President Aliyev was elected for a third term, and 2013 to 2,360, according to the London-based Foreign Policy Centre."

It was not until March 2014 when some of the country's most prominent individuals were put behind bars, incarcerated on dubious charges like those mentioned above. However, although officials in Baku thought they could get away with putting their critics behind bars, they were deeply mistaken. Not only have the arrests resulted in further criticism of the country's dubious rights record, but

Azerbaijan's economy has tanked, suffering from a sharp decline in oil prices. As a result, it became harder to maintain a spotless international image which was funded by petrodollars from abroad. It seems that the chapter is not closed, as it has become clear that there are in fact political prisoners in Azerbaijan after all.

By 2014 criticism of the country's human rights record reached such an unprecedented level that the United States Congress introduced a bill titled the "Azerbaijan Democracy Act", recognising Azerbaijan's human rights violations and its crackdown on freedoms. This act, the first of its kind, was a signal that international patience was starting to wear thin. Eventually, concessions would have to be made if Azerbaijan's leadership wanted to maintain friendly ties with countries like the United States.

Bargaining chips

Therefore, ahead of his visit to Washington DC for the Nuclear Security Summit in March-April 2016, Aliyev approved the release of 14 political prisoners. These included N!DA activists Rashadat Akhundov, Mahammad Azizov and Rashad Hasanov; bloggers Siraj Karimli and Omar Mammadov; former government official Akif Muradverdiyev; chairman of the National Statehood party Nemat Penahli; Musavat party activist Yadigar Sadigov; journalists Parviz Hashimli, Hilal Mammadov and Tofig Yagublu, and finally human rights defenders Taleh Khasmammadov and Anar Mammadli. Even so, deciding to relinquish some of Aliyev's most prized possessions did not mean much, especially given how little these recently released prisoners could actually do.

However, Aliyev did not release all of those identified as political prisoners, opting to keep a few of the more significant names in prison handy to be used as bargaining chips in forthcoming political endeavours. These names include journalists and bloggers Seymur Hezi, Nijat Aliyev, Abdul Abilov, Rashad Ramazanov, Faraj Karimli and Araz Guliyev, as well as political activists Fuad Gahramanli and Ilgar Mammadov. In fact, the full list is much longer and includes some 70 religious activists as well.

As investigative reporter Khadija Ismayilova (who was released on May 25th 2016 on a suspended sentence) wrote from her cell: "Aliyev needed these prisoners so that in exchange for their release, he could shake hands with Obama, or get a loan from the World Bank to finance his failing currency and crippled economy after the sudden fall in oil prices." She was referring to the release of the 14 prisoners. "Aliyev is shamelessly trying to use political prisoners as bargaining chips to advance his foreign policy agenda. Yet they are supposed to be happy that they were freed," she wrote. The piece was published in the *Washington Post* and was meant to serve as a reminder to the international public, including President Barack Obama, that Azerbaijan's political prisoners were not some kind of toys "to be exchanged for diplomatic gain by Baku or Washington".

However, there are fears that Khadija's calls are falling on deaf ears in western decision-making circles, something that would greatly benefit Azerbaijan's leadership. Despite the financial crisis, the drop in oil prices and two devaluations, the recent Panama Papers demonstrate that the country's leadership is still very rich and powerful, while its friends are still determined (as long as they are fully supplied) to continue lobbying on Azerbaijan's behalf. The country also remains a viable alternative energy transportation route for the West, bypassing Russia, whose unfriendly relations benefit Azerbaijan. The country is also a declared "loyal partner" in the US-led "war on terror".

> Despite the financial crisis, a drop in oil prices and two devaluations, the recent Panama Papers demonstrate that Azerbaijan's leadership is still very rich and powerful.

In addition, conspiracy theories feed paranoia that someone is out to get the president and overthrow the regime, which fuels further crackdowns. The regime's fears are so great that the authorities have accused most western-led international organisations of sponsoring a revolution. Every organisation that was under the magnifying glass of suspicion was kicked out of the country, while their local partners faced criminal investigations, interrogations, arrests and detentions. "Azerbaijan is among the top ten foreign governments buying influence in Washington", wrote Ilya Lozovski in his piece investigating Azerbaijan's lobbying ventures in the US. "In addition to traditional diplomacy, it has advanced these messages through aggressive lobbying in the think-tank world, in state legislature and in the halls of Congress."

Revolving door

While the exact number of remaining political prisoners varies according to various reports, it is safe to say that Azerbaijan is operating a "one in, one out" policy. On May 10th 2016, Bayram Mammadov, a member of the youth movement N!DA whose final four members were released just two weeks before, was detained on suspicion of painting graffiti that said "Happy Slave Day!" in Azerbaijani (a play on the phrase "Happy Flowers Day"). The graffiti appeared on a statue of former president Heydar Aliyev. Celebrated every year on May 10th, Flowers Day is Azerbaijan's national holiday. It also coincides with the birthday of Heydar Aliyev, the late president and father of Ilham Aliyev. Apart from Mammadov, police detained Giyas Ibrahimov, a member of the leftist youth group SolFront, on similar charges.

Both young men have reportedly been tortured while in detention and threatened with rape by police batons. "They beat me harder and demanded that I accept the charges. They swore at me and insulted me. They took my pants off and threatened to use a bat on me 'immorally' – that is, to rape me. I had no choice but to accept the charges, confess and sign the testimony that was handed to me," Mammadov wrote in his testimony. In another case, on June 22nd 2016, the court in Baku extended the pre-trial detention period of another political activist named Fuad Gahramanli. Gahramanli, the deputy chair of the Popular Front party, has been under arrest since December 8th 2015, with no official charges having been brought against him since that time.

> In its relations with the West, energy and security prevails, while democracy and human rights are secondary.

At the end of the day, Azerbaijan has the best of both worlds. At home, it has created a system where no checks and balances exist and the ruling elite hold a monopoly over power and key stakeholder positions. Elections are marred with fraud and the media scene is far from objective. Non-governmental organisations face draconian laws and mass criminal investigation. In its relations with the West, energy and security prevails, while democracy and human rights are secondary.

There is a clear need to put an end to the "business as usual" policy towards Azerbaijan and expose the illegal and corrupt nature of the Aliyev regime for what it is. It is time for an international reassessment of Azerbaijan's human rights record, before we have even more "Denisovichs" imprisoned in the country. NEE

Arzu Geybullayeva is an Azerbaijani columnist, blogger and journalist.
She is also a visiting fellow at George Washington University.

I chose not to be afraid

A conversation with Rasul Jafarov, an Azerbaijani lawyer and human rights defender who was arrested in 2014 and sentenced to six and a half years. He was pardoned in March 2016. Interviewer: Agnieszka Lichnerowicz

AGNIESZKA LICHNEROWICZ: What was it like being behind bars in Azerbaijan? Were you afraid? Journalists have been killed there...

RASUL JAFAROV: I was not afraid. The risk exists and it does not matter whether you are in or out of prison. I chose a path and I chose not to be afraid. Of course, tomorrow, it may change. I could be blackmailed or my family could be threatened. That could change my mind.

However, I do want to say that sometimes I hear criticism that sending books to prisoners or organising flashmobs in front of embassies is not enough. Yet for somebody in prison, and everybody will confirm this, it means a lot. In a prison, you are in psychological turmoil. No matter how strong you are, it is a struggle with yourself. You doubt your actions and wonder why you should waste your youth there. The prison guards try to use these moments and try to break you. The letters and demonstrations of support on the outside help both morally and psychologically, they strengthen you.

Where do you get your energy from? Why did you get involved?

Many people ask me this question. When I was in prison, the other prisoners and guards were even asking me why I do it, why I do not go to work for British Petroleum or some other big company in Azerbaijan. To be honest, I still have no direct answer. I think I just fell in love with human rights during my studies.

Maybe it also came from my family. I remember when I was in school, my grandmother convinced me to listen to Radio Liberty, the BBC and Voice of America. Now, I am in too deep to leave. I feel that I have a responsibility to my country. I love Azerbaijan. I love Baku. We have good food, sun, the Caspian Sea and wonderful people. I was born there.

Why do you think you were pardoned and released?

I was released together with 16 other people. I think it happened largely because of the domestic economic situation; the government needs to be on good terms with western countries, especially the United States, and international financial institutions. Azerbaijan needs loans and credit. Nevertheless, I think it is wrong. We are against trading people for deals. We demand a halt to politically-motivated arrests. As long as they continue to happen, the West should cease any dealings with Azerbaijan…

This sounds a little unrealistic…

Maybe. Sometimes you need to have idealistic views, especially if you are a defender of human rights in Azerbaijan.

What would you expect from European countries?

I would ask them to at least raise these issues as part of their relations with the regime in Baku. They do not even have to do so publically; raising them privately is sufficient. Unfortunately, we know that countries do not do so, despite the fact that they like to present themselves as human rights supporters. Even so, if human rights are too much to force on the regime, they could at least push for greater economic freedoms.

Baku has become known for its highly effective lobbying and diplomacy. Do you think that European governments are more aware of that today?

The regime has spent a lot of money creating a positive image of itself. A special phrase has even been coined for Azerbaijan: "caviar diplomacy". It describes all the methods used to buy representatives and MPs from the Council of Europe, the European Parliament and other institutions to silence the criticism. However, due to the economic situation, the regime is unable to spend so much now…

How do you argue against realpolitik supporters who say that Europe needs a regime in Baku to fight terrorism and produce oil?

If the situation in Azerbaijan does not change, it is very possible that the terrorists will come to power here as well. If the government controls the media and arrests opposition activists, other groups will arise. There are already others in Azerbaijan and whilst I still believe that fundamentalist thinking is not popular, that can change. Frankly speaking, it is unpredictable. If western powers want Azerbaijan to have real political and economic stability in the future, they simply cannot ignore human rights.

Do you think that the current economic crisis may change people's support for the regime?

Of course, the regime was and still is supported by many people. Despite that, I think the crisis is starting to impact opinions. People are afraid to talk about it publicly, but they do so in their kitchens, as they did in the Soviet Union, or on Facebook. At the same time, I think this process is slow.

Photo courtesy of Rasul Jafarov

"In a prison, you are in psychological turmoil. No matter how strong you are, it is a struggle with yourself," says Rasul Jafarov, an Azerbaijani lawyer and human rights defender was arrested in 2014 and released in March 2016.

Whilst reporting on the president's family finances, journalist Khadija Ismailova was blackmailed, threatened and finally imprisoned. We also know more about President Ilham Aliev's businesses thanks to the Panama Papers. How does this influence people's opinions?

The finances and business practices of the president's family are nothing new to the people of Azerbaijan. The Panama Papers were not shocking to them and corruption is part of our daily lives. Some people even agree that high-ranking officials should have villas.

Some people in the West argue that countries like Azerbaijan are not ready for democracy?

We have had experience with democracy. We had a democratic, parliamentarian republic from 1918 until 1920. Women had the right to vote in Azerbaijan before they did in France, the US or Sweden. On the other hand, we are now seeing regression rather than progress. In the 1990s Azerbaijan was more democratic than it is now and we had more freedoms. That is why I dismiss the argument that in their relations with Azerbaijan, other countries should give the regime more time because we are a young democracy.

What is the best scenario?

First of all, the government should create space for alternatives and organise free and fair elections. Some people are critical about the opposition because they remember the 1990s, when the opposition was in power, but we now have new people on the political scene and new faces in the opposition. I do not believe that we can change this ugly system with the current government. If they agree to a transformation, they will lose power.

However, slowly increasing the number of freedoms and allowing alternatives to take power would lead to change.

Do you believe that in your lifetime you will be able to talk as openly as you are now in the Azerbaijani media?

I believe it. I am an optimist. I have to be. NEE

Rasul Jafarov is a lawyer and prominent human rights defender in Azerbaijan. He was arrested in 2014 and later sentenced to six and a half years in prison. He was considered a prisoner of conscience by Amnesty International. He received a pardon in March 2016. He is currently based in Prague.

Agnieszka Lichnerowicz is a Polish journalist and a foreign desk chief at the radio station *Tok FM*.

Central Asia's opposition: Go directly to jail

Do not pass go

PETER LEONARD

Five nations in Central Asia emerged from the rubble of the Soviet Union, only to enjoy the briefest of flirtations with political diversity. Throughout the 25 years since Kyrgyzstan, Kazakhstan, Tajikistan, Turkmenistan and Uzbekistan gained independence, jailing political opponents has become a commonplace.

Out of all the Central Asian states, the most dispiriting recent development has come from Kyrgyzstan, a mountainous and largely rural nation often held up as the region's "best candidate for democratic evolution". In July 2016 all eyes were on the Supreme Court, when the three presiding judges were set to rule on a case concerning the country's most high profile jailed inmate. In the interests of clarity, it might be better to describe Azimjan Askarov not as a political prisoner but rather a prisoner of politics.

The 65-year old activist made a name for himself in his native southern town of Bazar-Korgon for his defence of local residents against the excesses of the police and prosecutors. Askarov's group, which he called *Vozdukh* ("Air") in acknowledgement of the importance of civil liberties, was unusually successful in embarrassing local judges and law enforcement authorities. One particularly egregious case successfully pursued by Askarov involved the jailing in 2007 of two people for the murder of a woman who turned out to be alive and well in neighbouring Uzbekistan.

Intimidating circumstances

In June 2010, as the country's hapless and newly installed leaders were struggling to deal with the fallout of their successful removal of President Kurmanbek Bakiyev, the south was gripped by bloody ethnic unrest. The minority Uzbek community in cities like Osh and Jalal-Abad felt the brunt of the violence at the hands of Kyrgyz mobs. In Bazar-Korgon, on the third day of turmoil, policeman Myktybek Sulaimanov was savagely beaten to death by what witnesses described as a large group of Uzbek men. Two days later, Askarov was pulled over in his car, carted off to a police station and later charged with Sulaimanov's murder.

Askarov's trial was held three months later, as nationalist Kyrgyz sentiments were still burning with white-hot intensity. Although most of the several hundred people killed in the ethnic violence were Uzbeks, police mainly targeted Uzbeks themselves with aggressive house raids and arrests. The south of Kyrgyzstan is a foreign country to most people in the capital, Bishkek, which is separated from the north by tall mountains. Most people there unthinkingly accepted the implied official narrative that Uzbeks were ultimately responsible for the troubles.

Against that backdrop, Askarov stood little chance of receiving a fair trial. Witnesses who were questioned in court created an image of Askarov that few of his colleagues, both in Kyrgyzstan and beyond, could reconcile with the gentle-natured grandfather and artist that they knew. Askarov, the witnesses told the court, was the bloodthirsty head of the mob that killed Sulaimanov and gave explicit instructions to kill as many Kyrgyz as possible. The trial was held in intimidating circumstances, with Sulaimanov's family and colleagues verbally and physically abusing the defence team throughout the hearings. A life sentence was inevitable.

Since that time, as Askarov's health has steadily deteriorated in the damp and cramped conditions of his cell, the government has bristled at international criticism. President Almazbek Atambayev, alive to the politically charged implications of revisiting any aspect of the ethnic unrest, has used harsh language to condemn Askarov and stand by the original verdict against him.

Askarov was finally thrown a lifeline in April 2016, when the UN Human Rights Committee issued a statement demanding his immediate release. Stung by the strength of the statement, Kyrgyzstan's Supreme Court made the surprise decision to review the case, although all appeals have technically run their course. However, at a hearing in July, the hopes of Askarov supporters were dashed again as the judges rejected a plea for his release and offered only the slim consolation of allowing a fresh legal review. The decision was widely described as a failure for a country that prides itself on its democratic credentials. "It's a missed opportunity for Kyrgyzstan to do the right thing by finally releasing a man who should never

Photo by: Kerri-Jo Stewart (CC) commons.wikimedia.org

Independence day celebrations in Turkmenistan, a hermit nation sitting atop one of the world's largest reserves of natural gas and where political prisoners tend to disappear into total oblivion.

have been jailed in the first place," Anna Neistat, director of research at Amnesty International, said in a statement following the Supreme Court ruling.

Inconvenient individuals

Kyrgyzstan's lurch toward illiberalism, which goes beyond the Askarov case, comes against the backdrop of a prolonged phase of economic stagnation in the region that has dampened prospects for political liberalisation. Kazakhstan, a far larger and richer country that lies north of Kyrgyzstan, has availed itself of costly public relations advice to forge an international image as a modern and reformist state. Unfortunately, much of those efforts were swiftly undone when the government reacted to a wave of protests in the spring of 2016 against contentious proposed land reforms by adopting a punitive approach.

In July the country's security services announced that they were investigating businessman Tohtar Tuleshov on suspicion of fomenting and funding the anti-reform rallies, which they said were his attempt to seize power. The accusations have provoked much incredulity, not least since Tuleshov has been in jail pending investigation on corruption charges since January. This episode is particularly baffling, since Tuleshov has no record of being especially critical of the government. However, the strategy of linking inconvenient individuals with outbursts of mass public discontent is one that has worked for Kazakhstan in the past.

In the middle of 2011, oil workers in Zhanaozen, a remote town in western Kazakhstan, declared a strike in a bid to get management at the state-owned energy firm KazMunayGaz to raise their salaries. Their cause was eagerly taken up by critics of the government. Among them was Vladimir Kozlov, the leader of an unregistered political party called *Alga!* ("Forward!"). The industrial action saw labourers squatting in Zhanaozen central square in a tiring war of attrition. Workers had their salaries suspended and a big bite was taken out of KazMunayGaz's profits.

Then, on December 16th, while President Nursultan Nazarbayev was basking in Independence Day celebrations in the capital, almost 2,000 kilometres east of Zhanaozen, the sit-in descended into chaos. Strikers later said authorities sparked the unrest by provocatively trying to hold raucous, jubilant festivities next to where the penniless workers had erected their encampment. At least 14 protesters were killed as police tried to put down the unrest.

Kozlov was in the business capital, Almaty, as the trouble unfolded, but he quickly resolved to make his way out to the west in an effort to mediate. On December 17th, several flights to the west of the country from Almaty were cancelled, a fact I recall well as I was one of several journalists trying to reach Zhanaozen that day. Despite this, the final scheduled plane of the day did leave, so the next morning, I and a few other reporters hitched a ride in Kozlov's van from the city of Aktau. Departure was delayed by a couple of hours, as Kozlov insisted on trying to file a formal report with the local police station to declare his intent to travel to Zhanaozen. One police station turned him away and another only agreed to accept a handwritten note. Before we could get to Zhanaozen, our van was stopped at a police checkpoint and Kozlov was asked to leave the vehicle.

The next time I saw Kozlov was the following September, sitting in a courtroom cage at his own trial, accused of whipping up the violence in Zhanaozen. Again, according to the prosecutors, the purported aim of this conflagration was said to be that of toppling the government. Kozlov defended himself against the charges with extended monologues, arguing that his advocacy activities on behalf of the striking workers would be considered par for the course in regular democratic systems. It was all for nothing. He was found guilty and sentenced to seven and a half years in jail.

Kozlov's fate highlighted a recurrent practice in Kazakhstan's dealings with its political opponents. If you cannot get the man you want, get his allies instead.

It has been widely speculated that *Alga!* and some allied anti-government media outlets were funded by Mukhtar Ablyazov, an exiled former minister and embittered Nazarbayev foe. Ablyazov fled to London in 2009 before being accused of stealing billions of dollars from one of the country's largest banks, although it was clear that his primary offence had been to dabble in opposition politics. At times during Kozlov's trial, it appeared as though it was Ablyazov who was truly in the dock. Prosecutors in the Aktau court described the disgraced businessman as the head of an extremist and criminal enterprise.

During our drive toward Zhanaozen, I pressed Kozlov about the rumours of his dealings with Ablyazov, but he responded coyly, allowing only for the fact that in a political scene as asphyxiating as that of Kazakhstan, compromises were required. In an unexpected development, rights activists announced on August 4th 2016 that Kozlov had been granted parole – his first lucky break after four and a half years of detention. His release was slated for later in the month.

Hard-core brand of authoritarianism

In Tajikistan, an impoverished nation bordering Afghanistan whose main exports are the hundreds of thousands of manual labourers its sends to Russia, the opposition understood the need to accommodate its expectations with the country's political reality. The Islamic Revival Party of Tajikistan (IRPT) was permitted to register as a political party on the eve of the collapse of the Soviet Union. In the maelstrom of the immediate post-independence period, the party joined forces with the variegated and improbable alliance of regional and ideological interests that consolidated to oppose an emerging ruling class of lapsed communists backed by warlord types.

A war between those two fronts ended in 1997 with a peace agreement designed to ensure an almost one-third quota of government posts earmarked for the opposition, of which the IRPT was the primary exponent. For years, the government tolerated the IRPT, if only slightly. The party could only ever win two seats in the 63-member lower house of parliament, despite boasting broad support among the electorate. For its part, the IRPT watered down the religious aspect of its political agenda and was firm but cautious in its criticism. Muhiddin Kabiri, a clean-shaven businessman who led the party from 2004, eschewed calling for protest rallies in evident concern of eliciting a disproportionately harsh crackdown.

> In Tajikistan, the opposition understood the need to accommodate its expectations with the country's political reality.

Seeing no proper opposition to his rule, President Emomali Rahmon steadily consolidated his power and unstitched the terms of the 1997 peace agreement. That process reached its culmination after an alleged attempted coup d'etat in September 2015 by a disaffected deputy defence minister. The speculation in the Tajik capital, Dushanbe, after that purported uprising was that there had not been a revolt at all and that the authorities simply exploited their own concocted reports of armed political unrest to embark on more political crackdowns.

Kabiri had already sensed the threat and committed himself to indefinite exile abroad. Less than two weeks before the alleged coup attempt, the remainder of the IRPT leadership summoned a press conference about how the authorities had locked them out of their own headquarters. They had hoped to hold the event in the Sheraton, but they were turned away by management in the hotel, which by coincidence happened to be hosting Gen. Lloyd Austin, commander of the US Central Command, at the time.

Inevitably, 13 leading IRPT figures were arrested in the middle of September 2015 on charges of being involved in the purported uprising. Less than nine months later and after a trial held behind closed doors, the Supreme Court sentenced the two deputy party leaders, Mahmadali Hayit and Saidumar Khusaini, to life in prison. Another 11 members of the party's political council received jail terms ranging from two to 28 years. The verdicts have cemented Tajikistan's embrace of the profound and hard-core brand of authoritarianism familiar to countries like Uzbekistan and Turkmenistan.

Cheap price

In a reversal of its characteristic behaviour, however, Uzbekistan bucked the trend in November 2015 by releasing a former member of parliament with the now-defunct opposition Erk political party, Murad Juraev. That the dissident had languished 21 years in jail on cooked-up charges of plotting to overthrow the government is highly indicative of the harshness with which Uzbekistan treats its political prisoners.

This sudden bout of clemency came just after a visit to Uzbekistan by US Secretary of State John Kerry, prompting cynics to suggest that President Islam Karimov was simply trying to curry favour with Washington. Uzbekistan's foreign policy consists of, in crude terms, maintaining equidistant relations with all its main interlocutors: Russia, the United States and China. Thus, Juraev's release as an utterly broken man was a relatively cheap price for buttressing that front. Juraev's original prison term was in fact repeatedly extended on spurious grounds, so that nine years became 21. This tactic has been adopted for opposition figures still believed to be in jail.

Human Rights Watch, which closely monitors the fate of political prisoners in Uzbekistan, has said that Muhammad Bekjanov, the editor of the Erk party newspaper, has been in prison for 16 years and had his sentence extended for supposedly breaking prison rules. Azam Farmonov, a rights activist jailed on extortion charges in 2006, was due for release in April 2016, but has had his prison term increased by a further five years. A steady drip of reports of chronic ill-health among those jailed in Uzbekistan on political grounds, for their activism, for doing journalistic work or for their religious beliefs trickles out into the public domain.

In Turkmenistan, a hermit nation sitting atop one of the world's largest reserves of natural gas, political prisoners tend to disappear into total oblivion. A typical case is that of former Foreign Minister Boris Shikhmuradov, who began to show signs of dismay at the idiosyncratic rule of late President Saparmurat Niyazov even while he was still in post. After begging repeatedly to have his request for resignation accepted, Shikhmuradov was given an ambassadorial post in China in early 2001. Dissatisfied with that, Shikhmuradov headed to Moscow, where he joined the ranks of the opposition.

> In Turkmenistan, political prisoners tend to disappear into total oblivion.

How he ended up back in Turkmenistan is the subject of conjecture. The government account is that he smuggled his way back into the country and took part in the plotting of the attempted assassination on Niyazov in November 2002. In scenes reminiscent of Soviet show trials of the 1930s, after his capture he was paraded on television to read a patently coerced confession in which he admitted to betraying his country and being the head of a criminal enterprise. That was the last time anybody has ever seen or heard of Shikhmuradov, who was only one of a countless number of people scooped up following the claimed assassination attempt.

When Niyazov suddenly dropped dead of heart failure in late 2006, it was hoped his successor Gurbanguly Berdymukhamedov might usher in a period of political openness. During a visit to the US in his first year in office, he gave a speech at Columbia University where he faced perhaps the only open question-and-answer session he will ever have to endure. Asked about Shikhmuradov, the president expressed certainty that the former minister was still alive, but offered nothing else.

The mystery that surrounds prisoners like Shikhmuradov prompted foreign-based activists from the Turkmenistan Civic Solidarity Group to start a campaign called "Prove They Are Alive!" NEE

Peter Leonard is the Central Asia editor for EurasiaNet.

Beyond control

Interview with Irina Borogan, deputy editor
of the Russian portal agentura.ru.
Interviewer: Evgeny Klimakin

EVGENY KLIMAKIN: To begin with, can you explain the difference between today's Russian security agencies and those of the former Soviet Union?

IRINA BOROGAN: First, it is important to say that the governments are different. The Soviet Union was a totalitarian state which supressed and controlled everything. At the moment, Russia is an authoritarian state. Many people like to compare Putin's Russia with the USSR, but the authorities currently control only certain groups. We have not reached the stage of total control just yet.

There was one main intelligence agency in the Soviet Union, the KGB…

Now we have a whole network of intelligence and security agencies. The FSB is the main successor to the KGB, but it is not as powerful. It does not have as many functions as the KGB had and nor does it have as many staff or as much power. Nevertheless, the methods and approaches the FSB has adopted are very similar to those used by its predecessor in Soviet times.

What are the similarities?

The similarities are everywhere. The security agencies actively seek an enemy and do not want to comply with the law. Basically, their aim is to enhance their own power. However, there is one important difference. Regardless of the fact that the KGB was very powerful, it was under the control of the Communist Party of the Soviet Union. In every KGB unit, there was a party cell that oversaw it operations. In the Soviet Union, the party was above the KGB. Now, the agencies are uncontrolled. Even parliamentarians do not have the right to ask anything of the FSB and they cannot force them to answer any questions. There have been instances where members of the parliament have submitted their questions and received a reply: "you do not have access to state secrets".

What about the head of state?

Theoretically, the agencies should be controlled by the president of Russia and the General Prosecutor's office. However, they are huge organisations with many subdivisions in every region of the country and it is virtually impossible to know what is happening everywhere. How can Vladimir Putin know what is happening in the FSB in Vladivostok, Buryatia, etc.?

Do you know how many people work for the FSB?

According to some estimates, it is about 200,000 people. This is unofficial data, since such figures have not been made public.

Is the recruitment of new people to the security agencies as active it was in the Soviet times?

Indeed, they actively infiltrate opposition movements. There was even a case where an agent was installed in the United Civic Front opposition movement. He later fled Russia and began to talk about what his employment in the security service was like.

And how does the FSB work with its agents?

The aforementioned example of Alexander Novikov is a good illustration of this. The employees of security agencies recruit agents and offer moderate material rewards. Novikov was meant to report on what was happening within the opposition movement: when new actions were going to take place, who they

were going to choose as their leader, etc. Perhaps they recruit people through fear, or by blackmail and criminal threats. All these methods are plausible.

In the Soviet Union, reporting on others was common. People wrote denunciations of each other and the security agencies happily used them. Is that the case today?

Unfortunately, the practice of denunciations has returned to Russia. People denounce university lecturers or representatives of civil society who express oppositional views. In our country, even parliamentarians have begun to write denunciations, although the security agencies do not need them in order to find their targets. They know whom to attack: opposition politicians, factions of the opposition that are not controlled by the authorities, non-governmental organisations and all those who think differently.

A group of men recently threw a cake at Mikhail Kasyanov, an opposition leader. It was claimed that this was done by "Chechen-looking people" who shouted "You – the shame of Russia!" I also recall a situation when milk was tossed at another oppositionist, Aleksei Navalny, in Anapa. Were the security services behind these actions?

When it comes to Kasyanov, it was probably organised by the Chechen leader, Ramzan Kadyrov, who regularly talks about his loyalty to the Kremlin and Putin. Chechens are very useful for carrying out such actions. Whilst you can blame a lot on Kadyrov, it is all inspired by the

Photo courtesy of Irina Borogan

government. Public attacks are also often co-ordinated by patriotic youth organisations like "Nashi" and the "Young Guard". These are pro-Kremlin youth movements which support Putin's policies, take part in various governmental campaigns and demonstrations, spread propaganda and fight against the opposition. They were created in order to form an active pro-Putin street force.

You are known for your investigations into Russia's security services. Do you feel an aversion towards them?

I have long worked as journalist and I have had to deal with a number of difficult topics. For instance, I have had to report on acts of terrorism. I wrote about

dozens of victims, wars and crimes and I learnt not to approach my work from an emotional perspective. Otherwise, one is simply unable to do a good job. Even so, in some instances, it is difficult not to react.

Can you tell us more…

For example, Beslan was very difficult. On September 1st 2004, terrorists stormed a local school there and took more than 1,000 children and adults hostage during a siege. The heads of the security agencies arrived, had a consultation which took a couple of hours and then quickly left. After that, the tragedy unfolded, an explosion took place, the school was stormed and hundreds of people died. However, the heads of the services were no longer there. The head of the FSB, Nikolay Patrushev, and the minister for internal affairs of Russia, Rashid Nurgaliev, had left for Moscow. They did not have the courage to face the people, look them in their eyes and say something. Of course, such situations spark anger and disgust.

Which agencies are more ruthless: the current Russian crop or the old Soviet ones?

In the Soviet Union, their control was total. Under the previous system, I would not have been able to discuss such matters with you with a recorder switched on. I would not even have been allowed to leave the country. I would have been put in jail for expressing the views and opinions that I am now. I write, give talks and travel abroad. That is the difference between a totalitarian system and an authoritarian one.

Do you believe that Russia's first president, Boris Yeltsin, wanted to depart from KGB standards?

When he set up the new Russian security services, Yeltsin initially looked to the United States as an example. He split the KGB into separate agencies and wanted each one to deal with a separate issue. An effective system of control over all the security services was never created. Instead Yeltsin decided to rely on competition between the different agencies. In 2003 Putin implemented a huge reorganisation of the security services. The border guards were merely absorbed by the FSB. Once the most powerful rival of the FSB, the communications agency was divided up between the FSB and the Federal Protective Service, which guarded Kremlin leaders. Under Putin's jurisdiction, the FSB was also given an upper hand over the ministry of internal affairs, the FSB placed counter-intelligence officers in key posts in the ministry. As a result, the FSB became more like the Soviet KGB.

Is it worthwhile comparing the Russian security services with their corresponding organisations in western countries?

It would definitely be rather difficult to compare them. In the US these organisations are overseen by Congress and the rule of law is respected. Yes, security agencies there also breach human rights, but a citizen can then go to court

and prove his or her case. In Russia, this would be pointless. There was a case when the private phone conversations of the opposition leader, Boris Nemtsov, were published on the internet. They appeared on the web site of *Life News* (a website with strong links to the Kremlin – editor's note). Nemtsov, having understood that only the FSB could have intercepted his conversations, went to court, but no one investigated the case. This is the main difference between our security agencies and western ones. Intelligence organisations everywhere, in every country, want to increase their power, but in Russia, they are beyond control.

How big is this mess?

Russia's security agencies could break the law as often as they like. Let me give you another example. A parliamentarian from Yekaterinburg named Maksim Petlin organised some protests in his city, and became a subject of FSB surveillance. Protesters expressed their anger against the Kremlin policies, including the FSB expanding power. His phone was then tapped, and the FSB received a warrant to eavesdrop on his conversations. The warrant stated that it was issued on the basis of the fact that Petlin had criticised the authorities and the FSB. It was a clear breach of human rights, a breach of an individual's freedom to express their opinion. He went to court, but it changed nothing.

There was also a case regarding a human rights advocate from Nizhny

Novogrod named Sergey Shimovolos. A few years ago, he noticed that wherever he went, he was being stopped and searched. He tried to take his case to court but the court simply stated: "Yes, you are almost certainly being watched because you are on a database of potential extremists." This, despite the fact that he had never been tried and had never committed an offence. His only "crime" was that as a human rights advocate he travelled around Russia and collected information about violations. Yet the security agencies put his name in the database along with the names of murderers, rapists or drug dealers.

Can Russian security agencies put anyone in prison?

They do not need "anyone". They are interested in those who have exceeded the limit for what is allowed, such as those who express oppositional views.

However, recently, the boundary between what is allowed and what is not has been blurred. Even just a couple of years ago, people who dared to criticise the Kremlin on the internet were not prosecuted. That changed a year ago, when the authorities began putting people in jail for writing posts critical of the Kremlin. Now, dozens are jailed for posting content on social media. Some of them did not even write anything. They simply re-posted material that someone else had posted.

I recall a case regarding activist Rafis Kashapov who was sentenced to three years in prison for publishing posts on social media criticising the annexation of Crimea...

Yes, publically expressing such opinions is no longer permitted. But such bans are issued by the Kremlin. The security services just enforce them. NEE

Translated by Agnieszka Pikulicka-Wilczewska

Irina Borogan is a Russian investigative journalist and the deputy editor-in-chief of the Russian portal *agentura.ru*. She is co-author of the book *The Red Web*.

Evgeny Klimakin is a journalist with TVN, previously working for Polish Radio.

Why Russia does not retrench

A revisionist but economically declining power may opt for retrenchment to replenish its domestic sources of power. This is not the path that crisis-stricken Russia is pursuing abroad as there is a strong belief among the Russian elite that regardless of economic difficulties, the country should behave like a great power.

Russia has recently been described as a "downshifter", a state that is rapidly falling behind its global competitors. There are good reasons for this. Its GDP is contracting for a second year in a row, putting greater distance between the top ten biggest economies in the world and Russia. Fixed-capital investments are shrinking, citizens' real incomes are melting and poverty is on the rise. Deterred by high inflation and a weak rouble, fewer migrant workers are venturing to Russia than before. To compound this situation, Russia's brightest minds are abandoning their motherland in growing numbers.

Although the roots of the economic slump are mainly internal, the downshift has been visibly precipitated by Russia's revisionist behaviour abroad. Instead of assisting domestic modernisation, Russia's foreign policy has inflicted additional damage to the economy (e.g., sanctions and counter-measures). At the same time, Russia has been sending ambiguous signals regarding a potential drawdown and re-engagement with the European Union and United States in what appears, on the surface at least, to be some level of retrenchment. Nevertheless, a more thorough inspection of the elite's thinking, the dynamics of the Russian economy and the role foreign policy plays in domestic politics reveals that the messages coming out of Moscow are "siren calls" that will likely lead to the wrong conclusions and precipitate misguided policy responses. Russia's revisionism is not a passing summer shower; it is a monsoon, with the cold wind marking a long-lasting shift in the weather.

> Russia's revisionism is not a passing summer shower; it is a monsoon, with the cold wind marking a long-lasting shift in the weather.

The perils of pulling back

Russia and its imperial predecessors have pursued retrenchment in the past. Quite often, this was dictated by sound military defeats and exacerbated by economic backwardness. At the same time, there is an inbuilt aversion among the Russian elite towards retrenchment, which is often post-factum interpreted as a betrayal of national interests. Until today, neither Mikhail Gorbachev nor Boris Yeltisn has been vindicated in Russia, partially because they presided over a deep drawdown from abroad.

There is a powerful belief within the Russian establishment that regardless of economic difficulties, Russia should behave like a great power abroad and actively nourish great power awareness within its society. This outlook was succinctly summarised by former foreign minister Yevgeny Primakov, who rhetorically asked his interlocutor, journalist Leonid Mlechin: "[...] are you not glad that in times when we have to beg for loans, we are taken seriously in international affairs and that many things depend on us? Is this contrast not important for our country, so that our people can feel like citizens of a great power?"

This stance has been reconfirmed by Russian elite polls conducted in 2016 by Hamilton College, which reveal that despite their nation's economic troubles, an overwhelming majority of Russia's elite (82 per cent) support an expanded version of national interests that stretches beyond its borders. For the first time since 1993 the elite displayed a preference for the use of military force as a foreign policy tool over economic statecraft.

For Russia's current leadership retrenchment symbolises weakness and is the surest path to squandering its great power reputation and international standing, which it recovered during the 2000s. It is anticipated that a pullback would invite more external pressure, rather than diminishing it. Moreover, rather than stamp out the domestic decline, it is feared that retrenchment will speed it up, as was case with the Soviet Union. President Vladimir Putin's assertion in 2004 that "the weak are always beaten" reflects the leadership's anxiety to show any sign of indecision or hesitation. Thus, it seems that there is a consensus that even if Russia is blocked militarily in one region, it should use alternative levers to keep targeted states under pressure. This explains the low-scale violence, cyber-attacks and economic coercion that was applied against Ukraine. Similarly, when Russia has been halted in one region, it should punch back with lesser costs in another. Russia's intervention in Syria (September 2015) during a relative lull on the Donbas front is clear proof of this strategy. For the reasons listed above, there are not yet many signs of Russia's deep disentanglement in foreign policy matters. Even if some recent behaviour or declarations fit the retrenchment paradigm, it would still be misleading to think that Russia is downsizing its external exposure. The intervention in Syria perfectly illustrates Russia's tactics, when a declared pullback (March 2016) sharply contrasts with what is actually happening on the ground.

The economy will muddle through

Previously, Russia had reluctantly wound down its combative foreign policy to focus its resources on overcoming economic backwardness. This pullback was regarded by decision-makers as a necessary step to replenish its resources for a renewed cycle of great power competition. Instead of calling it retrenchment, Russian diplomats preferred to describe it, in 19th century terms, as "concentration". Despite the fact that many current economic indicators are in the red zone, the scale of the crisis is not devastating enough to dramatically alter Russia's power calculations and thus push it towards another wave of top-down modernisation. After a substantial GDP reduction of 3.7 per cent in 2015, the decline is expected to slow down this year to 1.9 per cent. Moreover, the Russian leadership believes that the economic contraction will be neither deep nor long.

These assumptions are based on three factors. Firstly, one of the principle sources of budget revenue, oil exports, has contributed to a slightly upbeat mood. Oil prices recovered from less than 27 US dollars per barrel in January 2016 and stabilised at around $40–50 per barrel range in late May that year. At the same time, Russia's oil exports grew by almost five per cent in the first half of 2016. These in turn should help to attenuate the fiscal pressure that Russia's budget is reeling from. Secondly, although the sanctions enacted in March 2014 have caused Russia's sovereign funds to visibly dwindle (by $62 billion), Russia still has enough money ($112 billion, equal to 9.3 per cent of GDP in 2016) to shore up almost two years of budget deficit. Thirdly, there are international forecasts which predict that modest economic growth in Russia will resume in 2017, while inflation will temper down. Therefore, Russian decision makers are increasingly beginning to think that the worst is behind them. There might be ups and downs, but the situation, in their view, has stabilised. Russia's Central Bank's decision to cut the key rate for the first time in almost a year is proof of regained confidence. The fact that the Russian economy has thus far resisted the huge double pressure mounted by the economic sanctions and the precipitous decline of oil prices since 2014 reinforces this outlook in Moscow. Thus, the conclusion drawn by the Russian leadership is that pugnacious foreign policy is doable, in spite of the immediate economic costs it may generate.

All this does not mean that that structural problems hampering Russian growth have suddenly evaporated and that the country will bounce back spectacularly as it did after the 2009–10 global financial crisis. However, there is a belief in Moscow that with cuts and the mobilisation of some additional domestic resources, the economy will be able to muddle through. In search of funds, the Russian government is squeezing state companies to pay more dividends into the budget, mulling limited privatisation and planning higher domestic borrowing. Russia is also undergoing executive cuts and delaying the financing for big projects in order to save money (e.g., power gas pipeline from Siberia to China, or the bridge to Crimea). The state is also partially shifting the burden onto the shoulders of citizens by making cuts to healthcare (oddly, national security and defence were spared from deep cutbacks) or increasing the domestic tax rates on gas and diesel. Finally, Russia hopes that the EU, consumed by the Brexit, will falter and will not be able to muster consensus to extend sectoral sanctions after they expire in January 2017. This should bring some relief to Russia's cash starved economy.

Slowing the downshift is what the Russian leadership is betting on, regarding the economy in the short term. Looking around, the ruling elite sees uncertainty in the EU and US about the sustainability of economic growth, as well as a deficit of political will to convert economic resources into power. In this situation, Russia, fully aware of its economic weaknesses, is trying to compensate by utilising its recovered military capabilities in a more decisive way, backed by forceful diplomacy. Hence, the "concentration" must wait.

Island of stability

Since 2014 Russian foreign policy has played an increasingly important role in its domestic politics. From a stabiliser in the early 2000s to an effective manager in the mid-2000s, in 2014 Putin became the captain of a battleship navigating unfriendly waters. As Russia enters a key electoral cycle (parliamentary elections 2016, presidential elections in 2018), domestic deliverance of increasingly militarised foreign policy is too attractive to be ignored by the top brass during the campaigns. There is a clear desire to partially blunt the effects of economic decline and nourish the feelings of great power status by revelling in Russia's recuperated military might. According to this logic, revisionism overseas should help prolong the status-quo inside Russia. Hence, instead of extricating itself from international involvements, Russia will probably be even more inclined to engage in provocative actions aimed at steering low-cost crises abroad, as well as creating more cracks in Europe's struggling order.

With no big economic accomplishments to trumpet, foreign policy issues could be used to mobilise, scare and distract. State-owned mass media outlets, which to a large degree shape public opinion, will serve as the main transmitters of these messages. The world around Russia is likely to be depicted as an area of chaos, chronic conflict and instability. In this context, the relative economic stabilisation and absence of major conflict inside Russia will be oversold as a huge achievement. The aim is to lower citizens' expectations and make them more appreciative of the little that they still enjoy.

Besides presenting Russia as an "island of stability", the government will under-score the external origins of domestic economic problems and multiple security threats coming from abroad. In the last three years, Russia's list of enemies has become longer, while its circle of friends has grown smaller. For example, a recent survey measuring Russian hostility, conducted by the Levada Centre, recorded a substantial increase in enmity towards the US (+34 per cent) and Ukraine (+37 per cent). Germany, which had previously scored low on the list (three per cent in 2013), made it into the top ten, scoring 19 per cent in 2016. Turkey has also entered this group. It is noteworthy that in 2015, only one per cent of Russian respondents perceived Turkey as an enemy. One year later, this number has jumped to 29 per cent. This demonstrates the swift capacity of Russia's opinion shaping propaganda machine. Following apologies from Turkey for the downing of a Russian fighter jet, Russia fully exploited the images of a "humiliated foe" before switching to a more neutral portrayal. It is expected that NATO's increased defensive measures to protect its eastern flank will be presented to the Russian public as an offensive step in preparing for a sudden attack against the motherland.

The stimulation of external threat perceptions will go hand in hand with messages promoting the need for internal mobilisation, resilience and pride of the armed forces. To this end, the authorities will most likely further exploit the connections between past military victories and current foreign policy. In Russia's public opinion surveys, military power and its heroic past viewed as criteria defining a great power has steadily climbed over the last three years. During "Victory Day" celebrations (marking the end of what is considered in Russia as the "Great Patriotic War") in 2016, the Russian president unusually made a point of the heroism of workers, who contributed just as much as the soldiers on the battlefield, ultimately leading to the triumph of the Red Army. The parallels are unambiguous, as Russia's leadership increasingly frames its country as a "besieged fortress". The national military-patriotic movement "Youth Army", set up this year to target the young generation across Russia, is a logical continuation of the mobilisation approach that breeds and further entrenches belligerent attitudes in society.

Punching above its weight

Despite the economic decline, Russia has thus far defied the conventional wisdom that less resources will lead to a more constructive and benign approach to foreign policy. A sudden reversal of course is unlikely to happen soon. Therefore, there are several considerations for the EU and the US to ponder in their relations with Russia moving forward.

Unlike the Soviet Union in the late 1980s, which strived to safeguard the status quo via retrenchment camouflaged by a diplomatic charm offensive, Russia will continue to behave like a gambler that speculates momentum to gain as much ground as possible against the EU and US. Contrary to expectations, a Russia in the midst of a slow motion economic decline might be tempted to act in a more disruptive way than it might do otherwise. A more introverted EU and US will invite Russia to behave even more affirmatively.

> Contrary to expectations, a Russia in the midst of a slow motion economic decline might be tempted to act in a more disruptive way than it would have otherwise.

One-sided initiatives to engage and accommodate Russia (especially the phasing out of sanctions before the full implementation of the Minsk ceasefire agreement on Ukraine) will misfire, since the ruling elite will interpret them as signs of weakness. Conciliation will validate Russia's revisionism. Too much focus on minimising risks will prod Russia to multiply and expose the EU and the US to new ones. Attempts to compartmentalise relations with Russia will be met with ever increasing diplomatic efforts to intertwine conflictual issues with potentially co-operative ones. Linkages will be used to divide transatlantic allies and extract concessions without delivering much in return.

Russia's strategy of punching above its weight requires vigorous counter-measures from NATO and the EU, aimed at consolidating resilience from the inside. However, it is not enough to train to eschew Russia's blows. NATO should also improve its military capacity to respond to attempts at upsetting the power balance in the Baltic, Black and Mediterranean Seas. Decisions at the NATO Summit in Warsaw should be regarded as another step in pursuit of continuous adaptation to the risks and threats coming from Russia. The hard power component is vital for deterring that country from encroaching on members of the transatlantic community and curbing its options for disrupting the Eastern neighbourhood and the Middle East. Moreover, support for deep security reforms and aggressive anti-corruption drives in Eastern European states such as Ukraine, Moldova and Georgia should reinforce this deterrence. At the same time, the EU has to show patience and allow more time for the sanctions that have been imposed on Russia to work. Instead of speculating about softening sanctions, it is in the interests of the EU to focus more on enforcing them effectively.

At the same time, governmental and civil society channels of communication with Russia should remain open. Although various platforms should be used to understand Russia's intentions, dialogue should not allow Moscow to revert to "business as usual", a state of affairs that would suit certain entrepreneurial and political constituencies in Europe (e.g., the energy sector) a great deal. The narrow pursuance of immediate business interests in the midst of Russia's mounting challenge will probably lead to deeper fissures in the economic, political and security order that provided the environment for businesses and societies on both shores of the Atlantic Ocean to thrive. ᴺᴱᴱ⟩

Stanislav Secrieru is an independent analyst specialising in issues relating to Russia and post-Soviet region. He was previously a senior research fellow at the Polish Institute for International Affairs.

Wschód w Twoim domu bez większego zachodu

Roczna prenumerata TYLKO 70 zł.

Teraz przy zakupie prenumeraty papierowej prenumerata elektroniczna na dowolny czytnik: ipad, tablet, kindle - GRATIS!

Szczegóły na:
www.new.org.pl

Magdalena Grzebałkowska, reporter, non-fiction writer, nominated for the „Nike Literary Award" / fot. Michał Szlaga

all about freedom festival 10.

14–22/10/2016/GDAŃSK

Europejskie Centrum Solidarności / pl. Solidarności 1

aaff.pl / ecs.gda.pl

CONSEIL DE L'EUROPE
COUNCIL OF EUROPE
J. MIRÓ - Femme aux beaux seins (1969)

EUROPEAN SOLIDARITY CENTRE AWARDED WITH THE 2016 COUNCIL OF EUROPE MUSEUM PRIZE

On 19 of April 2016, the official Council of Europe Museum Prize award ceremony was held at Palais Rohan in Strasbourg. This year's laureate – the European Solidarity Centre – is the first institution from Poland to be ever distinguished with this prestigious award. The ceremony was attended by the President of the Parliamentary Assembly of the Council of Europe Pedro Agramunt, the Chairperson of the European Museum Forum Goranka Horjan and representatives of the city of Strasbourg. A speech on the phenomenon of Solidarność was delivered by the Deputy Prime Minister and the Minister of Culture and National Heritage of Poland Professor Piotr Gliński.

Representatives of the European Solidarity Centre brought to Gdańsk a diploma and the statue Femme aux beaux seins (Woman with Beautiful Breasts) by Catalonian artist Joan Miró, which will be displayed in the ECS Winter Garden through April 2017.

The President of the Parliamentary Assembly of the Council of Europe presents the statue by Joan Miró to Basil Kerski, the director of the European Solidarity Centre, during the ceremony in Strasbourg.
Photo: Magdalena Mistat | ECS

ME East EUROPE
WITH A VIEW TO THE FUTURE

date | **19-20 May 2016 Thursday-Friday**
venue | ECS, 1 Solidarity Square, Gdańsk
contact | europe@ecs.gda.pl

Sławomir Dębski – director of the Polish Institute of Foreign Affairs and Paul W. Jones – ambassador of the United States to Poland
Panel discussion: NATO IN THE 21ST CENTURY. HOW SAFE ARE EUROPEAN DEMOCRACIES?
Photo: Grzegorz Mehring | European Solidarity Centre

Patrycja Sasnal – expert on the Middle East, the Polish Institute of International Affairs and Lew Zacharczyszyn – Consul General of Ukraine in Gdansk
Panel discussion:
HOW HAS THE EUROPEAN UNION NEIGHBORHOOD POLICY CHANGED | DUE TO CONFLICTS IN EAST EUROPE AND IN THE SOUTH?
Photo: Grzegorz Mehring | European Solidarity Centre

Pawel Kowal – historian, politician, journalist, former Secretary of the State in the Ministry of Foreign Affairs and Rita Süssmuth – former president of the Bundestag
CONCLUDING PANEL DISCUSSION
Photo: Grzegorz Mehring | European Solidarity Centre

ecs.gda.pl

ambassador
of the new
europe

Organizers

european
solidarity
centre

Kolegium
Europy Wschodniej
im. Jana Nowaka - Jeziorańskiego
we Wrocławiu

WINNER

Serhii Plokhy
The Last Empire: The Final Days
of the Soviet Union
Publisher: Znak

Already in its fifth edition, the award "AMBASSADOR of the NEW EUROPE" is bestowed annually by the European Solidarity Centre and the Jan Nowak-Jeziorański College of Eastern Europe in Wrocław. The author of the best publication receives: a medal, a cash prize (worth 5,000 PLN) and the privilege to use the title "Ambassador of the New Europe".

This year the jury had to choose from 75 submissions which met the formal requirements. After several meetings, discussions and votes the jury decided to award Serhii Plokhy for his book "The Last Empire: The Final Days of the Soviet Union".

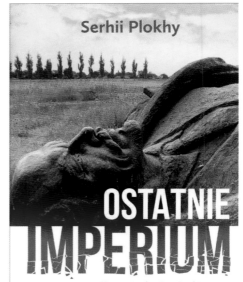

Serhii Plokhy

OSTATNIE IMPERIUM

Historia upadku Związku Sowieckiego

znak

International conference

THREE REVOLUTIONS.
PORTRAITS
OF THE
CONTEMPORARY
UKRAINE

27–28 February 2017
College of Europe, Natolin Campus

Registration and more info:
3r.natolin@coleurope.eu / www.coleurepe.eu

The conference is the culmination of a research project conducted by the College of Europe (Natolin) in collaboration with Harvard Ukrainian Research Institute, Canadian Institute of Ukrainian Studies, UCL, Mohylan Academy in Kiev and CNRS in Paris, Centre of East European Studies UW, Institute of Political Studies PAS. The goal of the project is to inspire a comparative analysis of three revolutionary moments in the recent Ukrainian history.

3R
THREE REVOLUTIONS

College of Europe
Collège d'Europe

Brugge

Natolin

WHAT SHOULD NATO DO?

What decisions will best serve peace?

How to reinforce public opinion support for the Alliance?

Follow us visegradinsight

VISEGRAD/INSIGHT

www.visegradinsight.eu

Tymoshenko still hungry for power

ROMAN ROMANYUK

Since Ukraine's last parliamentary election in 2014, the status of Yulia Tymoshenko in the Ukrainian parliament has changed substantially. She was initially part of the coalition that came to power after the EuroMaidan; now she has declared herself and her party to be part of the opposition. Since then she has become a staunch critic of President Poroshenko and as a result, has seen a steady increase in support for her party.

Yulia Tymoshenko is a heavyweight in Ukrainian politics. She has found herself in various situations since she entered politics. Despite the challenges she has faced, she has always found a way to advance her political goals. She was prime minister of Ukraine twice and her opponents tried to put her in jail the same number of times. Nevertheless, Tymoshenko remains a prominent figure in Ukrainian politics. Her influence on the state's decision-making process is now very limited because of a conflict with the country's leadership. However, support for her has been steadily rising in recent months, in the same way that it has for her party Batkivshchyna ("Fatherland").

The only thing preventing Tymoshenko from turning the support of the electorate into real political influence is that there are no upcoming elections to the Verkhovna Rada (Ukraine's parliament). According to opinion polls, if an election was to take place today, Tymoshenko's party could increase its parliamentary presence by a factor of three or four compared to what it has today. Calling an early election is now the primary goal of the Batkivshchyna party and its leader. However, since an early election would not be accepted by Ukraine's Western partners, including the United States and the European Union, Tymoshenko is pursuing a very cautious line. On the one hand, she has sharply criticised the current authorities and, on the other, she is striving to maintain normal relations with the West.

Tymoshenko returns

On February 22nd 2014 the former president of Ukraine, Viktor Yanukovych, fled Kyiv, heading towards Russia. On the same day the Verkhovna Rada adopted a new law releasing Tymoshenko, Yanukovych's main opponent, from prison. The general prosecutor's office, which was controlled by the former president, had initiated several cases against the opposition leader which had ultimately led to her imprisonment. Even if Tymoshenko had won any of those cases in the European courts, she would have been arrested on other charges. On February 22nd, when Tymoshenko was released from prison, she was immediately shuttled to Kyiv to join the protesters in Maidan Square.

When Tymoshenko gave a speech from the stage that had been erected in the middle of the square, many politicians and public activists who were leading the protests viewed her as a representative of the old system. Tymoshenko was a symbol of the opposition's struggle, but she also represented the system that brought Yanukovych to power. However, Tymoshenko did not see it this way. After two years spent in prison, she was keen to return to politics, preferably in a key position. Therefore, Tymoshenko's name was listed on the presidential ballot in the spring of 2014. Yet, Ukraine's western partners were sceptical. Officials from the EU and the US hinted that the country should rather be led by someone who represented a new generation.

> Tymoshenko was a symbol of the opposition struggle, but she also represented the system which brought Yanukovych to power.

Tymoshenko's decision to run for the presidency did not go down well with party members either. In the spring of 2014 a split was beginning to emerge in Batkivshchyna. It had been initiated by Tymoshenko's long-time allies and most trusted colleagues Arseniy Yatsenyuk, Arsen Avakov and Oleksandr Turchynov. They did not think that Tymoshenko would succeed and thus advocated the need to support a "single candidate", Petro Poroshenko. Furthermore, while Tymoshenko had been isolated from politics during her imprisonment, her former allies had managed to become prominent figures themselves. They did not want to return to the role of "junior partners" again.

The net result of all this was that Poroshenko won the election in 2014 based on 55 per cent of the vote. Tymoshenko came in second with nearly 13 per cent. This demonstrated two main trends. Firstly, this level of support reflected the impact she had had on the political situation in Ukraine after EuroMaidan. Secondly, the election result was the end of Tymoshenko's first era. She had gone from a person whose release was demanded by the most influential global leaders to becoming an ordinary Ukrainian politician.

Batkivshchyna's final split crystallised during the parliamentary elections in August 2014. A significant number of Tymoshenko's closest associates left the party and established the People's Front as their new political project. The primary reason behind the split was the race for prime minister, a position that Tymoshenko wanted to once again occupy. However, Arseniy Yatsenyuk, one of the EuroMaidan leaders, had similar ambitions. While Tymoshenko was in prison, Yatsenyuk managed to become an independent political player and gain the support of influential Batkivshchyna members. Therefore, Tymoshenko was forced to change the public perception of her as a politician from the old generation who was being left behind by all her young, progressive colleagues.

Electoral failure

In this way, a large group of young specialists, lawyers and engineers appeared on Batkivshchyna's voting list. Moreover, Nadiya Savchenko, the Ukrainian pilot who had been detained in Russia since 2014, was also included in first place on Tymoshenko's party ballot. Nevertheless, despite these political manoeuvres, Tymoshenko was unable to secure any significant electoral success. Victory in the parliamentary election went to Yatsenyuk's People's Front which, together with the Petro Poroshenko Bloc, won the majority of votes cast. The leaders of the People's Front notably got the top government positions: Yatsenyuk became prime minister, Avakov the minister of internal affairs and Turchynov became the secretary of the National Security and Defence Council.

Tymoshenko's party won a mere 5.7 per cent of the vote, which translated into 19 out of 450 seats in the Verkhovna Rada. Therefore, the Batkivshchyna faction joined the government coalition. However, it always took an independent position on all policy matters. Tymoshenko herself took every opportunity to publicly confront Yatsenyuk and President Poroshenko. As a result, Batkivshchyna pulled out of the government coalition in spring 2016 and joined the ranks of the opposition.

In doing so, Tymoshenko was able to boost her popularity by harshly criticising the authorities, although her influence over matters of state was significantly diminished.

Today, all key political decisions in Ukraine are made by several policy-makers. Traditionally, these include the presidential administration, the cabinet of ministers and the Verkhovna Rada. In the context of the undeclared war with Russia, the significance of the National Security and Defence Council has also risen, since it takes major decisions concerning military operations, the country's strategy and how the huge defence budget is allocated. Tymoshenko's main problem in this situation is that all of these positions are controlled by actors and people who are in long-standing conflicts with her.

The relationship between Tymoshenko and Poroshenko has never been perfect. Their disagreements go back to just after the 2004 Orange Revolution, when then President Viktor Yushchenko dismissed Tymoshenko's cabinet in the autumn of 2005 (Poroshenko supported this decision). Tymoshenko revealed to the media that when she was trying to persuade Yushchenko not to dismiss her cabinet, Poroshenko came into the president's office and called her political party "traitors". This conversation proved to be fatal for Tymoshenko's career in 2005.

No reliable co-operation

In 2014, as Poroshenko ran for president after EuroMaidan, casting himself as the "single candidate representing democratic forces", Tymoshenko invariably called him the "single candidate representing oligarchs" in her public statements. She implied that Poroshenko, with a personal fortune worth over a billion dollars, negotiated a division of the spheres of influence in the country with other Ukrainian oligarchs. This statement was supported by information that Poroshenko, together with another opposition leader, Vitali Klitschko, had held a secret meeting in Vienna with one of the most influential Ukrainian oligarchs, Dmytro Firtash, before the 2014 presidential election. Allegedly, an arrangement was made that Poroshenko would become president and Klitschko would be made mayor of Kyiv. This is exactly how subsequent events played out.

This information was revealed after the 2014 election, during a trial in Austria where US authorities were trying to extradite Firtash to the US on corruption charges. Poroshenko is very skilled at bargaining with his opponents behind the scenes. However, he does not really like being publicly insulted.

Although Poroshenko is very sensitive to Tymoshenko's continuous accusations, both politicians have shown that they are able to put aside their mutual insults and agree on key issues in critical situations. The most recent example of this was

Time for fresh ideas in Ukraine's democratisation efforts

NICHOLAS ROSS SMITH

Despite a reduction in the levels of corruption being the key message of the Orange Revolution in late 2004 and the 2014 EuroMaidan Revolution, neither were able to break the pervasive grip of oligarchs on Ukrainian politics. New ideas are needed to break this cycle. In pursuit of its democratisation, perhaps Ukraine should look to its own past rather than the West for inspiration.

It has been a tumultuous 24 months for Ukraine's government. Numerous scandals have cast serious doubt over Petro Poroshenko's stated objective, outlined at his presidential inauguration in 2014, to undertake democratic reform and fight corruption. In 2016 alone it was revealed that Poroshenko had an offshore holding company, his economic minister, Aivaras Abromavičius, resigned in protest and the much-maligned former Prime Minister Arseniy Yatsenyuk eventually quit as well (to be replaced by Poroshenko ally, Volodymyr Groysman).

Underpinning all of these scandals has been worrying democratic stagnation and, in some cases, backsliding in the areas of corruption, the rule of law, freedom of the press and increasing presidential power. Of course, this is probably not a particularly surprising outcome for anyone who has been following Ukraine's democratisation efforts since its independence in 1991 which represents 25 years of numerous false promises regarding democracy and its promotion.

Role of the elite

In truth, Ukraine faces numerous internal obstacles to achieving a functioning liberal democracy. The country's economy, which was significantly hit during the 2008 global financial crisis, has more recently taken a further turn for the worst with the ongoing crisis in the east and the destruction of the Donbas region, its industrial heartland. Thus, not only is Ukraine's economic outlook dire (a 12 per cent drop occurred in 2015), inequality is also on the rise (inflation reached 44 per cent for 2015), both of which do not bode well for its democratisation prospects.

In addition, although Ukraine's civil society is rated as functional (by democratic rating indexes such as Freedom House and Bertelsmann Stiftung) it clearly lacks the substantive critical mass necessary for organic democratisation to develop. Unsurprisingly, after numerous failed democratic movements have resulted in the rise of political apathy amongst the majority of average Ukrainians, few seem genuinely convinced that a democratic future for their nation is possible.

> After numerous failed democratic movements resulted in the rise of political apathy amongst average Ukrainians, few seem genuinely convinced that a democratic future for Ukraine is possible.

However, while the aforementioned issues are problematic and certainly need addressing, if successful democratisation is to be achieved, the biggest internal hurdle is undoubtedly rectifying the role of the elite in Ukrainian politics. According to Jean Grugel and Matthew Bishop, democracy is not "a question of waiting for economic conditions to mature or the political struggles unleashed by economic change to be won". Instead, it is the outcome of intentional actions pursued by the elite. In the context of the transitions that have occurred in the independent states that emerged from the Soviet Union's collapse, all of which have ostensibly attempted some level of democratisation, the role of the elite has been important as to whether democracy has developed or not.

Popular mobilisations demanding democracy, such as those which occurred when the Soviet Union collapsed or during the colour revolutions, as well as more recently in Ukraine in 2014, have often grabbed international attention. However, Henry Hale argues that in the majority of post-Soviet states, "political contestation is at root an elite affair where powerful groups compete to manipulate mass opinion through biased media and machine politics". Therefore, the elite are arguably the most important variable when understanding the democratisation trajectories of post-Soviet states.

The influence of Ukraine's elite on their nation's politics and governance in its two and a half decades since independence has been significant. Initially, in the early years of independence under the first president, Leonid Kravchuk, the Ukrainian political elite was mostly made up of former high-ranking figures from the communist apparatus. However, due to wide-ranging economic reforms, especially privatisation, implemented when Leonid Kuchma came to power in 1994, a new breed of elite emerged in Ukraine: the oligarchs.

The term oligarch, in this context, refers to business magnates who acquired huge amounts of wealth, often through criminal connections or activities, during the privatisation process. The rise of oligarchs, occurring at a time when economic and political transitions were failing, was clearly bad for the development of democracy in Ukraine. Beyond the obvious problems, which included rising corruption (Transparency International documented worsening perceptions of corruption in Ukraine), Paul Kubiček argues that the rise of oligarchs undermined the potentially positive impact of trade unions, which could have reverted the "over-centralisation of authority and lack of checks on both political and economic power".

Breaking the system

Despite reducing corruption being the key message of the Orange Revolution in late 2004 and, more recently, the 2014 Euromaidan Revolution, neither were able to break the pervasive grip of oligarchs on Ukrainian politics. Therefore, unlike during long periods of Kuchma's presidency or Vladimir Putin's rule in Russia, it is apparent that the oligarchisation of power has reached a point where the president is impotent in the face of oligarchic interests.

> Despite promises to de-oligarchise Ukrainian politics, President Poroshenko's rule has illustrated that history is once again repeating itself in Ukraine.

Unfortunately, the momentum generated by the EuroMaidan movement seems to have been co-opted by Poroshenko and his oligarchic supporters, since none of the key grassroots figures in that movement were represented in positions of any real power under the new regime. As a result, despite promises to de-oligarchise Ukrainian politics, Poroshenko's stint in power has illustrated that history is once again repeating itself.

Ultimately, as Henry Hale observed during the Orange Revolution, the current political system in Ukraine, whose design has not been significantly altered by the ongoing Ukraine crisis, means that rather than moving towards democracy or autocracy, power will merely perpetually vacillate between competing elite groups, creating cycles of "regime behaviour". Therefore, breaking this embedded system, which exists solely to serve oligarchic interests, appears to be the key challenge impeding Ukraine's prospects for achieving greater democratisation from within. Indeed, without significant changes to the amount of political power possessed by the oligarchs, then regardless of what happens in any other sphere of democratisation (i.e. civil society growth, elections, the rule of law) a western-style democracy in Ukraine is largely impossible.

Sadly, during Ukraine's 25 years of independence, there has been little evidence to suggest that a fully functioning western-style liberal democracy is within reach. However, a more pertinent question is whether Ukraine should aspire to achieve one. Indeed, as the former Communist Central Eastern Europe and Baltic countries, which undertook putatively successful democratic transitions in the 1990s and early 2000s (with significant help from the EU) demonstrate, a western-style liberal democracy is undoubtedly preferable to the illiberal, even kleptocratic, democracy Ukraine currently has. However, as the people of Hungary probably attest to, reaching some magical threshold in the transition from communism to democracy does not guarantee a utopian outcome. Instead, it brings with it other democratic challenges, ones for which the West currently does not seem to have any answers.

The inherent problem with the western-style democratic system Ukraine has long been trying to achieve is that it is a representative system which eschews the more substantive areas of democracy, particularly direct citizen participation and deliberation, for the more modest goals of having free and fair elections and a functioning rule of law. Any system which has elections as the centrepiece of its popular participation inherently suffers a mix of populism, party partisanship, interest group influence, the bombardment of campaign slogans and propaganda and political apathy, all of which combine to reduce the role of the demos in the democratic process. The United States' forthcoming 2016 presidential election illustrates this point vividly, as there are unprecedented levels of partisanship, populism and campaign bombardment in the Clinton versus Trump race, all of which is making a mockery of the ideals that are supposed to underpin democracy.

Outside the box

In classical Athens' golden age (5th century BC), elections were seen as a fast-track to oligarchy (rule by a small group of elite). Aristotle, in Book Four of his seminal treatise *Politics*, stated: "that all offices are filled by election is one of these oligarchical characteristics; that the power of inflicting death or banishment rests with a few persons is another". Furthermore, in a quote that will worry many witnessing the rise of Donald Trump, Aristotle argues that "history shows that almost all tyrants have been demagogues who gained the favour of the people by their accusation of the notables".

Looking across the globe, it is not hard to discern oligarchic traits in most western democracies. Recent headline-grabbing studies have asserted that the United States (by Martin Gilens and Benjamin Page) and the United Kingdom (by Ferdinand Mount), two bastions of western democracy, are closer to oligarchies than democracies as, in reality, average citizens can rarely directly influence policy. Additionally, due to the rapid rise of inequality across the West, many political systems are actually teetering on the verge of becoming plutocracies, reducing the role of average people still further.

Therefore, if Ukrainian people really want democracy, perhaps their inspiration should not be the modern western understanding of democracy but rather democratic ideas that are firmly outside the box. In this regard, Ukraine can look to its past. Indeed, the country was the setting for a remarkable social experiment that occurred roughly between the 15th and 18th centuries: the Cossacks.

The Cossacks, not to be confused with the modern manifestation of the term, who can currently be found on both sides of the front lines in Donbas, were bands of people that ventured into the frontier lands of southern Ukraine in order to seek out an existence away from the control of the Polish–Lithuanian Commonwealth or the Tsardom of Russia. Given that the Cossacks were ostensibly driven by a desire for freedom and abhorred the injustice of serfdom under the Poles or Russians, they quickly became Ukraine's first advocates for democracy.

As Cossack communities grew from their small and inauspicious beginnings, their central desire for liberty led to the adoption of democratic systems as their primary form of governance. The most prominent of the Cossack settlements, the Zaporozhian Sich, gradually became something of a democratic republic, as its highest authority was an assembly known as the Sich Rada. In other words, the Sich Rada was a governing committee that was comprised of all Cossacks and was charged with day-to-day decision-making in the settlement, including decisions on when to go to war or make peace. Indeed, key positions, such as military leaders (the highest being the Kosh Otaman, later called the Hetman), were directly elected, but it was only in exceptional circumstances, such as war, that these leaders gained executive powers.

The Zaoirizhian Sich's democratic ideals ran so deep that in 1710, one of its most famous figures, Hetman Pylyp Orlyk, wrote a constitution which effectively guaranteed the separation of powers between the legislative, executive and judiciary branches of government, predating Montesquieu's more famous The *Spirit of the Laws* by 38 years. Article VI of the Constitution stated that: "The present Hetman, and his successors, shall consult these general officers, colonels, and general councillors concerning the integrity of the fatherland, its common weal, and all public affairs, and shall not undertake, establish and execute anything through his personal authority without their prior advice and consent."

An inspiration

The example of the Cossacks is not without its caveats, particularly when it is used as an inspiration for democracy. Undeniably, the characterisation of the Cossacks presented above is an overly romantic version, as in reality, there were times when things were less than democratic and quite illiberal. For instance, despite originally having Jewish members, the Cossacks were responsible for numerous massacres against Jews in the 17th century and the liberty and democratic principles at the heart of their movement (which were already limited to just men) gradually gave way to authoritarianism.

Whilst it is important to acknowledge these realities, they should not detract from the didactic potential of the Cossacks as a base for a new democratic ideal in contemporary Ukraine. The Cossack desire for emancipation from the controlling elite is arguably the same desire that drove swathes of people in Ukraine to the streets to protest the corrupting role of the elite on their country and resulted in the two revolutions that took place in 2004 and 2014 respectively. However, whereas the Cossacks were able to break free from the control of the elite, contemporary Ukrainians have not been able to do so in either of their post-independence revolutions.

> The Cossack desire for emancipation from the controlling elite is arguably the same desire that drove huge swathes of people in Ukraine to the streets to protest in 2004 and 2014.

This is where the Cossack's democratic history can serve as an inspiration for Ukraine moving forward. While Ukraine is currently attempting to guarantee the necessary separation of powers for a functioning democracy, it should also attempt to create an assembly which more closely reflects the essence and functioning of the Sich Rada. The democratic appeal of the Sich Rada was that because Cossack communities were so small, everyone could participate in the assembly, giving all citizens a direct and deliberative role in their democracy. Clearly, facilitating the participation of all citizens is impossible in a country the size of Ukraine (whose current population is 45 million people), so instead, it must, like all representative systems across the world, use elections to appoint a reasonably sized assembly of 450 members known as the Verkhovna Rada (the parliament). However, as stated earlier, elections are easily corruptible and, as is glaringly obvious in Ukraine's case, tend to lead directly to oligarchy.

The ancient Greeks faced a similar problem, as their analogue to the Sich Rada, the Ekklesia, often comprised of as many as 40,000 individuals. Understanding that so many people would complicate decision-making and aware of the pitfalls of elections, the Ekklesia used a lottery system called sortition to randomly select members to sit in the Boule, a council which prepared the agenda to be discussed by the Ekklesia, and in the Heliaea, a court which judged legal infringements. Elections were only used to select magistrates who presided over military, economic and societal affairs, but these were strongly scrutinised by the Boule and Heliaea.

Sortition was an important component of the Athenian ideal of democracy as it enabled input from a fair cross-section of society, not just the elite. However, it should be noted that only certain men could be citizens in Athens. Nevertheless, as the famous Greek scholar Herodotus argued: "The rule of the people has the fairest name of all, equality (isonomia), and does none of the things that a monarch does. The lot determines offices, power is held accountable and deliberation is conducted in public."

Could such a method reinvigorate Ukraine's push for democracy? If one agrees with the central thesis of this article, that oligarchs are the biggest detriment to democracy and the democratisation process in Ukraine, then a system which involves all Ukrainians and minimises the influence of one of the most corruptible aspects of democracy, namely elections, would undoubtedly be a positive development.

The challenge is to break free from the control of the elite (not just a problem for Ukraine, it should be stressed); something which the previous two revolutions might have achieved if an alternative model had been feasible. The irony is that if Ukraine could somehow channel the Cossack spirit and undertake reform towards a uniquely Ukrainian democratic pathway based on the principles of the Sich Rada, it would quickly move from being the laughing stock of democracy to actually presenting an alternative model for other languishing pseudo-democracies to follow. NEE

Nicholas Ross Smith is a visiting scholar at the University of Auckland's politics and international relations department (New Zealand). He is currently finishing a book on the conflict in Ukraine, which will be published by Edward Elgar later this year.

Helpless in their own homeland

IGOR SEMYVOLOS

The period between March and June 2014 was a crucial time for the Crimean Tatar national movement. The events which took place then have determined the fate of the Crimean Tatars under the current Russian occupation, as well as resolving the Tatar issue in the long term, both in occupied Crimea and mainland Ukraine.

Recalling the events of February 26th 2014 near the Crimean parliament in the city of Simferopol, Refat Chubarov, the chairman of the Mejlis of the Crimean Tatar people, emphasised the need to strike a balance on that difficult day. The situation felt overwhelming. "We were convinced that we had managed to save Crimea," Chubarov had said. At that time, the joint efforts of the Crimean Tatars and Ukrainian activists had prevented the commencement of an extraordinary session of the Crimean parliament and it seemed that the leadership of the parliament had agreed on an arrangement that would resolve the political crisis.

The situation changed dramatically on February 27th, as Russian special forces seized the Crimean Parliament and Council of Ministers buildings. They subsequently held a session at gunpoint, where the decision to hold a "referendum" and join Russia was adopted. Although it is fair to say that Russian aggression against Ukraine had already begun on February 20th when the occupation started, February 27th was, without a doubt, the day when the global spotlight was shone on this aggression and made it clear, both to Ukraine and the rest of the world. The Crimean Tatars were helpless in the dramatic events that were unfolding.

Retrospective view

With some exceptions, the Crimean Tatars did not have any influence on the decision-making process in the autonomous republic because the policy of the previous government, the "Macedonians"*, was designed to oust the Crimean Tatars from power. A short period of co-operation between Vasyl Dzharty, the chairman of the council of ministers, and the Mejlis representatives was an exception to the rule. The following period, from March to June 2014, was crucial for the Crimean Tatar national movement. The events which took place then determined the fate of Crimean Tatar institutions, the fate of the Tatars themselves under Russian occupation and the long term resolution of the Crimean Tatar issue, both in occupied Crimea and mainland Ukraine. Nevertheless, in order to better understand those landmark events, a retrospective analysis of the evolution of the Crimean Tatar issue over the last 20 years is needed.

On June 26th 1991 two months prior to the dissolution of the Soviet Union, the Second Kurultai (assembly) of the Crimean Tatar people was held in Simferopol, which restored its state-building tradition that dated back to the first Kurultai of 1917. In addition to establishing executive bodies the Kurultai adopted the Declaration of the National Sovereignty of the Crimean Tatar people, which proclaimed that the peninsula was the "national territory of the Crimean Tatar People".

Two months later, after the Moscow coup d'état failed and Ukraine proclaimed its independence, the leaders of the Crimean Tatar movement reached an agreement with Viacheslav Chornovil, the leader of the People's Movement of Ukraine, and began looking to Kyiv. Attempts to get the Ukrainian leadership to pay attention to their demands yielded little result. Amid preparations for the referendum on independence, pressure from Moscow and the growing secessionist sentiment in Crimea, Kyiv decided to place its trust in the loyal members of the Communist Party of Ukraine rather than leaders backed by 120,000 Crimean Tatars, who by that point had returned to their homeland in Crimea.

These factors predetermined how the situation would develop. The primary task for the Crimean Tatars at that time was to survive and to provide land, work and a livelihood for their compatriots, who were repatriating from Central Asia on a mass scale. This was all taking place in the context of active resistance by the Crimean authorities and amid flourishing Russian separatism. The silent restriction, according to which the Crimean Tatars could only live in the steppe areas

---

* Macedonians, *Makedontsi* in Ukrainian – (from Makiivka and Donetsk) is a nickname of the Donetsk group which came to power in Crimea after Viktor Yanukovych won the presidential election of 2010 and which was headed by the former mayor of Makiivka, Vasyl Dzharty.

of Crimea, led to massive squatting and clashes between the Crimean Tatars and military forces. It also led to frequent conflicts, resulting from the pursuance of a divide and rule policy, with Russian-speaking residents from the villages adjacent to the protest fields, which formed the so-called public order squads.

At that time Kyiv had a rather limited leverage over the situation in Crimea, which was on the verge of separatism. After the peninsula was reabsorbed into Ukraine's constitutional framework in March 1995 and the central authorities restored their control over it, Kyiv turned its attention to the Crimean Tatars, who had demonstrated their loyalty to the idea of a united Ukraine. During this period co-operation was developing, which eventually led to the legitimisation of the Mejlis as the representatives of the Crimean Tatars to the president of Ukraine. It is important to note that in the 1990s, the leaders of the Crimean Tatar movement remained in political coalition with the People's Movement of Ukraine and did not criticise the central government. Instead, they maintained a neutral position, focusing primarily on resolving their internal problems.

Orange Revolution and disappointment

The 2004 presidential election and the Orange Revolution forced the Crimean Tatars to publicly choose sides. They actively supported Viktor Yushchenko and expected that as president, he would support them on the peninsula. However, his support never came. During his infamous visit to Bakhchysarai in May 2005, Yushchenko, instead of thanking the Tatars for their support and granting them preferences, suggested that they repeal their declaration on national sovereignty. The Crimean Tatars expected that their representatives would be appointed as the heads of local administrations through open competition. However, Kyiv was interested in reaching a compromise with the local elite. Therefore, it was only partially able to meet the demands of the Crimean Tatars. As a result, two district administrations were headed by them, although one of those was symbolic, the Bakhchysarai district administration, chaired by Ilmi Umerov.

The governmental crisis in Kyiv following the 2006 parliamentary election, delays in resolving urgent problems and dissatisfaction with the "stagnant policy" of the centre in relation to Crimea provoked another notable confrontation: the events surrounding the central market/Kyrk-Azizler necropolis in Bakhchysarai. In many cases, the disturbances of August 2006 were an indicator of how the situation in Crimea would develop. For the first time, organised groups of Russian nationalists, alongside visitors from Sevastopol who had a distinctly military appearance, were ready to take forceful measures against Crimean Tatars (the majority of the

Russian nationalist participants later turned out to be active supporters of the occupation and annexation of Crimea).

Accordingly, based on the conclusions drawn from the events in Bakhchysarai
and particularly after the Russian-Georgian War in 2008, crucial efforts were made
to prevent destabilisation in Crimea and to avoid a direct forceful confrontation
between the Crimean Tatars and Russian nationalists. That approach, which was
supported by Ukrainian and international experts, should have prevented Russia
from any interference in Ukrainian internal affairs pursuant to the Georgian scenario. This aspect shall be taken into account when discussing the modus operandi
of the Crimean Tatars during the EuroMaidan Revolution and at the initial stage
of Russian aggression. Moreover, such ideas were prevalent for some time, even
after the onset of Russia's aggression. At the same time, the period between 2005
and 2010 was notable for the emergence of two new Crimean Tatar media outlets,
the ATR channel and Meydan radio.

Divergence

The already insecure status of the Crimean Tatars on the peninsula was further
weakened as Viktor Yanukovych came to power in Ukraine and the Donetsk team,
headed by Vasyl Dzharty, took over in Crimea. This period was also notable for
the structural changes that took place in the Crimean Tatar community. A group
of influential Crimean Tatar businessmen was formed and became involved in national Crimean Tatar politics. The connection between the Mejlis leadership and
the Crimean Tatar business community had always been strong and support for
business was one of the priorities of the national movement. The business-supported
initiatives of the Mejlis funded national events and activities. They also promoted
the development of a national identity. In turn, the Crimean Tatar businessmen,
with the support of the Mejlis, were granted political cover from excessive attention from various state authorities and security agencies. This symbiosis could
only work as long as the Mejlis remained an influential political player in Crimea.

This alliance began to fail during Yanukovych's rule. The faction of Crimean
Tatar businessmen who gravitated towards Remzi Ilyasov criticised the radical
positions of the Mejlis leadership, which identified itself as part of the Ukrainian
opposition. As the Crimean Tatar community grew more diverse, so did the breadth
of opinions within it. This included a proposal to change the procedure for electing
Kurultai members, as the idea of direct elections was becoming more popular. The
Mejlis leadership, who were used to serving a dual purpose, i.e. acting as a pressure
group and an executive body, faced the possibility of extending democratic proce-

dures and practices which would heavily impede their governance and decision-making processes. Tensions between the business group inside the Crimean Tatar national movement and the politicians were revealed at the first session of the Fourth Kurultai of the Crimean Tatar people in October 2013. Refat Chubarov, who at the time represented the politician's party, won the election to become head of the Mejlis against Remzi Ilyasov, with 126 votes to 114.

> Ensuring the support of the Crimean Tatars was important for Russia at the start, so it is no wonder they attempted to bribe them with the promise of a 20 per cent representation quota in government.

Ensuring the support of the Crimean Tatars was important for Russians during the initial phase of their aggression in 2014. Hence, there were attempts to bribe them with the promise of a 20 per cent representation quota in government, protection for the Crimean Tatar language and recognition of Kurultai-Mejlis institutions. All these promises were made prior to the "referendum" of March 16th and were designed to increase Crimean Tatar participation in it. However, overtures to the Crimean Tatars ended immediately after Russia's annexation. Inevitably, the Ukrainian parliament was unable to influence the processes taking place in occupied Crimea and as a conciliatory measure, adopted a resolution recognising the Crimean Tatars as indigenous people of Ukraine.

Soft collaboration

In late March 2014, almost immediately following the annexation, an extraordinary session of the Kurultai was held in the city of Bakhchysarai, discussing, among other issues, the modus vivendi of the Crimean Tatars under their new, extreme conditions of occupation. Notably, the leader of the Crimean Tatars, Mustafa Dzhemilev, who was not present as he was in Brussels at the time, had predicted that the Kurultai would decide to hold a Crimean Tatar referendum on the status of Crimea.

The occupying authorities were becoming aware of the threat of destabilisation and felt uncertain, since the first wave of the "Russian spring" had failed in other regions of Ukraine and Russia's best chance for direct military invasion had been wasted. The authorities did what they could to prevent the referendum. To this end, representatives of the Russian Republic of Tatarstan, as well as the muftis of Moscow and Tatarstan, met with the leaders of the Crimean Tatars. As a result, a

decision on the referendum was not made and a course of soft collaboration with their occupants was chosen instead. The figure that played a crucial role in the adoption of this decision was the Crimean Tatar businessman and owner of the ATR channel, Russian citizen, Lenur Islyamov. He soon became deputy prime minister of the occupational government.

The situation and sentiment of the Crimean Tatars changed drastically after the people's deputy of Ukraine, Mustafa Dzhemilev, visited Simferopol. The occupational government viewed his return very negatively. It was especially annoyed about the fact that Dzhemilev had ordered that the Ukrainian flag, which was removed after March 16th, should be displayed on the face of the Mejlis building in Simferopol.

"It is not merely a piece of cloth, it is a symbol. By taking down your flag, you surrender, and it is not right", Dzhemilev said in Simferopol. He caused more trouble for the occupational authorities, who were probably anticipating awards for their "domestication" of the Crimean Tatars, when he travelled to the administrative border between Ukraine and Crimea for a second time in early May. However, unlike in April, he was not granted permission to enter. The Crimean Tatars were waiting for him on the other side and after learning of the ban, they tried to help their leader cross the border.

It is worth noting post factum that the events of May 2016 hampered the occupants' plans for soft collaboration with the Crimean Tatars. Another explanation for why the occupational regime refused to co-operate with the Mejlis in late May is the events that were taking place in mainland Ukraine, where the hybrid war with Russia broke out and the authorities' intentions were to detach eight oblasts. In late May, Lenur Islyamov was dismissed from the Crimean government for "political bias". In this way, the period of peaceful co-existence between the occupying government and the Mejlis ended.

Switching sides

While the structures that comprised the national movement generally held true to their ideals and did not agree to openly co-operate with the occupants, only certain representatives of other Crimean Tatar organisations that were in opposition to the Mejlis-Kurultai followed suit. Almost all of the bodies that had previously co-operated with Yanukovych's Party of Regions sided with the enemy. Remzi Ilyasov, the former rival of Refat Chubarov for the position of the chairman of the Mejlis, was one of the first to side with the occupants and became the vice chairman of the a new "State Council of the Republic of Crimea". In total, four representatives of the Mejlis agreed to co-operate with the aggressor.

The case of Mufti Emirali Albayev is an apt example of this. The Muftiate, or the Spiritual Directorate of Muslims of Crimea (DUMK), is an important and legitimate Crimean Tatar community institution. The mufti is a permanent member of the Mejlis, unlike others who are elected at the Kurultai. Almost immediately following the occupation, the mufti was surrounded by counsellors from Russia, gently hinting at what he should do. To make it clear that they were serious, searches, detentions and the confiscation of religious books were conducted in a number of mosques that were under the control of muftiate.

Incredibly, these repressive acts stopped immediately after the mufti displayed his loyalty to the occupying regime. However, the Spiritual Centre of Muslims of Crimea (DCMK), or Tauric muftiate, was registered in Crimea using Russian registration data as far back as 2010. Back then, the DUMK viewed the DCMK as schismatic and constantly complained of "trickery" on the part of the Ukrainian special forces, which were allegedly involved in setting up the organisation. Following the annexation of Crimea, the DCMK was re-registered. Its activity, however, depended on the conduct of the mufti. After he publicly opposed the leadership of the Mejlis, the organisation was neutralised and co-opted into the muftiate. Although the views of the mufti evolved gradually, when it became clear that he had switched sides, it was too late. The last attempt to influence the mufti was made in Turkey, where Chubarov tried to speak with him. Unfortunately, he failed and today the mufti and the muftiate are under the total control of the occupying authorities.

Repression and persecution

Today, there are dozens of people in Crimea whose imprisonment is clearly politically motivated. Achtem Chiygoz, the deputy chairman of the Mejlis of the Crimean Tatar people, Ali Asanov and Mustafa Degemerdzhy remain detained as part of the events that took place on February 26th. At least four people have also been arrested in relation to their membership in the "Hizb ut-Tahrir", and their number continues to grow thanks to constant searches and arrests. As of May 2016, 18 Crimean Tatars have been arrested, of whom 14 are convicted of organising and plotting terrorist attacks. Pursuant to the decision of the prosecutor's office of the occupying authorities, the Mejlis of the Crimean Tatar people was recognised as an extremist organisation and banned in Crimea and Russia. Ukrainian organisations are also subjected to repression and persecution. The majority of them no longer have the right to operate legally on the peninsula. A repressive law is in force in Crimea which renders any opposition activity virtually impossible. The banning of the Mejlis has exposed a large number of socially active Crimean Tatars who were involved in the Kurultai-Mejlis system, particularly the members of local mejlises that were responsible for the development of the Crimean Tatar community.

The Ukrainian central authorities were helpless when Russia attacked and could not secure freedom for their citizens in the Autonomous Republic of Crimea. As a result of the occupation and annexation, they were forced to either flee from persecution or to get used to life under the occupation, an existence that is constantly plagued by danger. The Crimean Tatar people were left alone with the occupiers and because they are largely outnumbered, cannot actively resist them. Their main goal now is to preserve the institutions and people who are repositories of institutional memory and to try and develop their organisations in mainland Ukraine as much as possible.

The idea of declaring the Crimean Tatar national territory autonomous, something that was supported by the President of Ukraine, will be followed by an extensive debate involving all concerned parties regarding the future social order in Crimea and the new rules of the game on the peninsula once the Russian occupying forces leave. However, it is important to understand that Crimea will only be free following radical changes in the Russian Federation. This might sound improbable today, but one should remember that back in 1986, nobody expected that the Soviet Union would have collapsed just five years later. According to our estimates, a window of opportunity may be open between 2020 and 2025, and we will be actively preparing for it. NEE

> Crimea will only be free following radical changes in the Russian Federation.

Translated by Olena Shynkarenko

Igor Semyvolos is the executive director of the Kyiv-based Association of Middle East Studies, a think tank dedicated to the analysis of Ukrainian foreign and domestic policies with a particular focus on Crimea.

ZAMEK
NA WODZIE
WOJNOWICE

Wojnowice Castle

HOTEL - RESTAURANT - FUNCTION HALLS - CONCERTS
Just 7 kilometres outside Wroclaw

www.zamekwojnowice.com.pl

Resetting Georgia-NATO relations

EUGENE KOGAN

Following the 2016 NATO Summit in Warsaw, it seems clear that Georgia has little chance of being granted a Membership Action Plan. However, it is evident that a business-as-usual approach towards its relationship with NATO is ill-advised. Top officials from both Georgia and NATO now need to sit down for a serious brainstorming session to iron out their differences on difficult issues and set out new guidelines for relations going forward.

Georgian leaders, the minister of defence in particular, believed that their wish to obtain a NATO Membership Action Plan (MAP) would be granted at one of NATO's recent summits. However, the last eight years have exposed the eternal lack of consensus among NATO member states, starting with the infamous Summit in Bucharest where NATO's open door policy towards Georgia was proclaimed. They have also highlighted Georgian officials' exaggerated expectations and optimism about this issue. Following the 2016 NATO Summit in Warsaw, it seems clear that Georgia has little chance of being granted a MAP and, as a result, the country remains in limbo. Furthermore, were Georgia to be offered a substitute for a MAP by NATO, perhaps an Associated Partnership, it would not ease the feeling of disappointment or even betrayal inside the country.

The biggest question that remains unanswered by both Georgian and NATO officials is the nature of relations between the two after the Warsaw Summit. Will Georgian officials realise that Georgia is a close "partner" and not a NATO "member"? That the process of membership has come to a standstill and needs to be reinvigorated but lacks new content? Or will they continue to delude themselves, as has been the case over the last eight years, in order to not lose their spirit of optimism and maintain their country's Euro-Atlantic orientation? Will NATO speak with one voice and say loud and clear that the Alliance's open door policy towards Georgia has failed and that the door is, in reality, shut? Or will NATO's ambiguity continue as if nothing has happened?

Unanswered questions

Undoubtedly, both NATO and Georgian officials are frustrated by the situation, since NATO's words do not reflect NATO's deeds, while Georgia's expectations have failed to materialise. The implicit veto that Russia has over Georgia's desire to join the Alliance hangs over that country like the Sword of Damocles, despite repeated statements by western politicians and diplomats that Russia has no such veto.

Although Chancellor Angela Merkel, French President François Hollande and United States President Barack Obama said "no" to a Georgian MAP, European NATO officials have kept a low profile, failing to clearly articulate that Georgia's chances of receiving a MAP were, and still are, very low (likely close to zero). On the other hand, American NATO officials have been more forthcoming, since they have felt obliged to be frank, blunt and less constrained by political correctness.

The implicit veto that Russia has over Georgia's desire to join NATO hangs over Georgia like the Sword of Damocles.

On May 13th 2015 Kurt Volker, a former US Envoy to NATO, said that: "One day Georgia may become a NATO member, however, I would like to say that NATO is not discussing this issue at present." On October 6th 2015 Volker told *Voice of America* that: "I do not think that Georgia and Ukraine should expect to receive a MAP at the upcoming NATO Summit in Warsaw." Furthermore, as recently as April 22nd 2016, Douglas Lute, the US Envoy to NATO, told the Aspen Security Forum in London that: "There is no way we are going to get consensus any time in the near future on adding Georgia and Ukraine. In practical terms I do not think there is much additional room in the near term, the next several years perhaps or maybe even longer, for additional NATO expansion."

There is no doubt whatsoever that the European leaders' official political correctness hindered them when it came to speaking clearly on this crucial issue. At the same time, Georgian officials have made a grave mistake by not challenging

European NATO officials on the issue of a MAP or membership. By challenging them, the Georgians would have found out where both sides stand on the issue and would perhaps start to think differently. On the other hand, maintaining a calm and amicable position has not helped Georgia. In the end, their officials are left with plenty of unanswered questions and thus have a difficult task in trying to convey a clear message to ordinary Georgians.

Disappointment and anger

Bearing all this in mind, what can we expect from Georgian officials after the Warsaw Summit? Perhaps we will see bitter disappointment and even anger, similar to earlier statements made by Tina Khidasheli, the defence minister (Khidasheli resigned in early August 2016 – editor's note), who said: "If the answer from Warsaw is negative, you can take my word for it, and I hate to say it, but it will have an immediate implication for Georgia's election results." If that is the case, then this approach is not going to help Georgia. To blame NATO for domestic shortcomings and electioneering is unwise. A better implemented domestic agenda is one of the keys to potential positive feedback from NATO. This point has often been reiterated by NATO officials.

> To blame NATO for Georgia's domestic shortcomings and electioneering is unwise.

What Georgian leaders, including the defence minister, have to understand and acknowledge is that they were the ones who failed to revise their policies and relations with NATO over the last eight years. Today, they urgently need not just revision, which is long overdue, but a whole new way of thinking, a new approach and finally, a new understanding with NATO. On the other hand, NATO is likely to be very reluctant to admit that its consistent open door policy towards Georgia has failed. Even so, NATO has to realise that its open door policy, which successfully brought Albania and Croatia into NATO in 2008 and which has recently led to Montenegro being invited to join, cannot be equalled by granting Georgia a MAP and ultimately bringing it into the Alliance. The decision to grant Georgia a MAP means that the Alliance is ready to defend Georgia against Russia, even though Georgia is not yet a member. The threat of Russia attacking Georgia cannot be underestimated and is very real.

Defending Georgia remains the most difficult issue for the Alliance to unanimously agree upon. NATO pursues a very cautious approach towards Russia, not because it is afraid of it but because it understands that confrontation with Russia would require the support of the EU population, would be very costly and would

Georgian president Giorgi Margvelashvili (left) meets with NATO Secretary General Jens Stoltenberg. Defending Georgia remains one of the most difficult issues for the Alliance to unanimously agree upon.

create a heavy burden for the allied leaders to carry. These crucial points are neither explained nor understood in Georgia and, as a result, need to be conveyed and explained at length to both Georgian politicians and ordinary Georgians alike.

What is evident is that after the Warsaw Summit, the Georgian business-as-usual approach towards relations with NATO would be ill-advised. Both Georgian and NATO top officials need to sit down for a serious brainstorming session to iron out their differences on difficult issues and set out new guidelines for Georgia-NATO relations. Transparency aside, certain parts of these new guidelines should be conveyed to the Georgian public. They should receive a clear explanation as to why NATO has failed to bring Georgia into the Alliance over the last eight years. Jens Stoltenberg, the Secretary General of the Alliance, should clearly state that: "Yes, Georgia is our closest partner but is not a member, since the Alliance lacks consensus on that issue."

Being honest with himself and with the Georgian public will help mitigate the feeling of betrayal and disenchantment that Georgians are currently feeling towards NATO. Furthermore, Stoltenberg's statement would help counter Russia and Russian sympathisers in Georgia, who claim that: "We informed you Georgians all along that NATO was not ready to bring you in. You never believed us and clung to the hope that the indecisive Alliance would stick to the promise it made at the Bucharest Summit back in 2008. It is time to face the facts."

To start anew

Nevertheless, several key points outlined below should be taken into consideration when determining the best way to reset relations following the Warsaw Summit. First and foremost, Stoltenberg should state loudly and clearly that a MAP is obligatory for Georgia in order to counter comments made by Davit Usupashvili, the chairman of the Georgian parliament, and Tina Khidasheli, the now former minister of defence, who have said that: "We in Georgia do not need a MAP." It is also of the utmost importance that the North Atlantic Council (NAC), as the principal decision-making body of NATO, reinforces Stoltenberg's statement that a MAP is not just important but crucial for Georgia. Countries that receive a MAP are not simply Alliance aspirants, but official candidates for NATO membership. Thus, it is critical to emphasise the linkage between a MAP and membership to Georgian officials and the expert community in Georgia.

Second, discussions in Georgia about receiving a MAP should be toned down, de-politicised and the Georgian leadership should ultimately be sober-minded about the chances of Georgia quickly getting a MAP. Statements made by Khidasheli, including things like "I am not going to tone down demands" and "Georgia will demand membership at the Warsaw Summit," do not help Georgia's case. Furthermore, it puts off those allies who have not yet made up their minds about bringing Georgia into the Alliance.

Third, there is a notion in Georgia that "We Georgians are entitled". As a result of the country's progress in following NATO and EU guidelines in pursuing various reforms and strengthening democracy, Georgia feels that it deserves to get NATO membership. This sense of entitlement needs to be toned down. Georgian officials need to understand that in these challenging times that Europe faces they should take nothing for granted. Instead, there needs to be a long-term approach, based on patience and resilience, to withstand difficulties along the road. For those impatient Georgians who live in the shadow of a belligerent Russia, this is easier said than done. Nevertheless, both sides need to determine how to solve the issue of strategic patience. It should also be stressed that questions such as when Georgia will receive a MAP will be asked repeatedly.

Fourth, NATO constantly praising Georgian achievements (particularly in Afghanistan) whilst at the same time pouring cold water on that country's expectations confuse and exasperate Georgians. NATO's language of ambiguity is not understood by them, as they are a plain spoken people. Therefore, NATO officials need to be forthright.

Fifth, European and American NATO experts on strategic communications should form a link between NATO, Georgian officials and ordinary Georgians. This team of experts must have expertise in Georgian domestic, foreign and security policy and be capable of delivering concise and precise messages from NATO to Georgia and back. They also need to be fluent in Russian. This point is of utmost importance, since the team should debate NATO issues throughout Georgia, not just in the capital, Tbilisi. Knowing Georgian is an extra bonus but not a precondition. It is up to NATO and Georgian officials to agree whether or not one of the aims of this team is to counter Russian anti-NATO propaganda, as well as some of Georgia's political anti-NATO rhetoric.

> NATO's language of ambiguity is not understood by Georgians, who are plain spoken people. Thus, NATO officials need to be forthright.

There is no guarantee that these suggestions will be seriously considered by either side. However, without a new impetus in bilateral relations, Georgia has little chance of overcoming its impasse, while NATO's eternal lack of consensus will remain a stumbling block. The only winner in this situation will be Russia. In the end, acrimony and accusations may fly, but they do not help Georgia or NATO under the current, difficult circumstances.

Eugene Kogan is a defence and security expert affiliated with the Tbilisi-based Georgian Foundation for Strategic and International Studies.

A post-modern construct deprived of ideology

A conversation with Olga Sedakova, a Russian poet and translator. Interviewer: Masha Makarova.

MASHA MAKAROVA: Is what we have seen in Russia in recent years a sign that the country is adopting its own path?

OLGA SEDAKOVA: I think that we have been witnessing a huge step backwards. I could never have imagined that at the beginning of the 1990s we would get to this point. We seem to be heading not even to the Brezhnev years, but towards Stalinism. The political language used during the Stalin era has already appeared, such as the phrase "agents of influence". Something unthinkable is happening.

However, it seems that this is what the people need. On the anniversary of Stalin's death, people go to the Kremlin wall and lay red dianthuses on the leader's tomb. There are queues of people…

I think that Stalinists are still in a minority. In general, ordinary people think very little about this. However, I have been in this world for a long time and I have seen how the public change their views. During the Gorbachev period, everybody turned out to be liberal. They would say how they always hated the totalitarian system. Now, they are becoming Stalinists. As we can see, it is that easy. I saw how ordinary people behave, those who are not fully responsible for their own opinions and who change them easily. What we are witnessing now, of course, is horrifying. It terrifies me when a former hawkish atheist suddenly announces that he is an Orthodox Christian, the most orthodox of all. Now, because of mass propaganda, the majority of people feel the same way. I say majority since I believe the sociological polls which show 80 per cent (or more) support for Vladimir Putin. The Stalinists are marginal, but people are driven by nostalgia.

Are they the same "Soviet people"? Or, perhaps, during the last 16 years of Putin's rule, a new type of "Russian man" has formed – "Putin's man"?

"Putin's man" is, of course, an attempt to reincarnate the Soviet man, and not the late-Soviet man, but the man of Stalin's making, the man of the 1930s. While ideology was crucial to the "Soviet man", "Putin's man" is a post-modern construct deprived of ideology. It is a "Russian idea" he represents, which is in fact meaningless, as no one can define its main assumptions. It cannot replace the doctrine which had been imposed on the Soviet people since kindergarten. You cannot do this with a "Russian idea". Russland über alles – and that is all. And what to do with it? To persecute the "Russophobes"? That is why I feel like I am in an awful dream.

Is this a kind of parody of the Soviet Union? A parody on the outside and a tragicomedy in substance?

It is indeed absurd. Brezhnev-era socialism was also absurd, but this absurdity crosses all boundaries. What is interesting is that there is no rhyme or reason to it. Ordinary people understand very well that those in power are criminals, but for some reason, they accept it. I do not know why. Fear of change, perhaps. Or a sort of a very deep inferiority complex that Putin has manipulated; that we do not fit in the western world.

Are there journalists in Russia who, in your view, constitute an important voice in the current situation?

There are good journalists, but they operate mostly online. I will not give any names, but there are a few people who write very well. However, they write for an internet audience, which is a completely separate network of people. The internet commentary is read by the intelligentsia. There are people who think critically, but they are an absolute minority who do not amount to much. We are helpless and defenceless. For example, there are motions on Facebook. We sign petitions (sometimes more than one a day) in defence of a park, or a dorm for the blind or a monument. We constantly write petitions, though I am not sure to whom. Sadly, we cannot do much more than that...

Surely these actions are a sort of therapy to clear up one's own conscience? Like the 1968 Red Square demonstration (the protest of the seven) when people took to the streets, realising that they would not change anything...

Of course, everyone understands that. It is possible that some small things, the most trivial ones, can be achieved. All of a sudden, a shelter for the blind or for stray dogs is saved; it does happen. However, as I recently wrote on Facebook, "what are these petitions and who initiates them all? And from whom do we want to protect literally everything? What for?" There is this impression that the current rule is total and indivisible.

After the Crimean campaign, Alosha Avdeev, who lives in Poland, said in an interview that he feels that the government stole Russia from him. Do you share this feeling?

Photo by Michał Ramus, courtesy of Krakow Festival Office.

"Everyone understands that Russia's current path is steadily spiralling downwards, that the system which has emerged cannot change. What will serve as the driver for change? No one can say," admits Russian poet Olga Sedakova.

I do not want to shift all the blame on the authorities, because there is interaction between those in power and the population. It is true that the Russia we love is very difficult to see. It only can be found in individual people. The popular frame of mind is horrible, the tone is horrible.

What does this agreement between the authorities and the population consist of? In the past, Putin could guarantee high salaries and stability. Now, fridges are empty and prices are increasing. What compels Russians to tighten their belts and say they will survive?

I do not understand those people. They speak very proudly: "We will live poorly but it is great, as Crimea is ours!" This is the only benefit. Of course, the financial situation is deteriorating and many people are beginning to find themselves struggling. However, the situation is not yet catastrophic. People are getting used to living in this nightmare as long as they believe that it could be worse and that is what they fear.

Is this why they continue to fear the West?

No, it is simply convenient to blame the West if anything goes wrong, just like in Soviet times.

If we talk about the Soviet Union, some countries which were once a part of it managed to break free and follow their own path, such as Ukraine and Georgia...

These countries are also in a poor and difficult state. We can say that no matter what, they made a categorical step. However, when it comes to Ukraine, I would not be so sure. They have their own internal mess. Nevertheless, they took a step; to break with a past like theirs is very difficult. What is needed is a great willingness and understanding of one's ultimate aim. Unfortunately, the country currently lacks this understanding.

Do you think that Ukraine will not succeed on its chosen path?

If we compare with the "white (protest) movement" in Russia in 2011–2012, it was mainly an educated group of people who took to the streets. The Maidan Revolution in Kyiv represented the entire nation and all its social classes. Far more of the population demanded change. Nevertheless, there are also some who do not want it and they will have to decide between themselves, as in Crimea and Donetsk there are people who want

to protect their Soviet ways. It should be an internal matter.

Was there a real desire for change in Russia in 2011–2012?

It was a very pleasant time. I do not think that anyone thought then that it was a moment to take a decisive turn and that something big would follow. Even so, suddenly, it seemed that everyone was free and people trusted one another. We understood that we had common interests. There was a festive atmosphere, which was dramatically and cruelly interrupted.

Was it the intelligentsia's game?

No, it was a genuine act, but people did not ask each other how far they were ready to go. It is one thing to come out and then leave; it is quite another to build barricades. At that time no one was willing to build the necessary barricades.

What will be the catalyst for real change in Russia?

I do not think anyone has the answer to that yet. Everyone understands that Russia's current path is steadily spiralling downwards, that the system which has emerged cannot change. What will serve as the driver for change? No one can say.

People who protest in Russia, for instance in Manezhnaya Square, are seen as foolish. Apart from a narrow circle of associates, no one takes them seriously and their voice is not heard...

As we have seen, a protest only has personal significance. There are people who cannot accept reality and, in order to preserve their own dignity, they express their feelings through protest. They do not necessarily hope that anything will come of it. However, there is now a different conversation taking place, one conducted with the language of force. Force applies everywhere. Next to my house, there is a park called Dubki, which we are trying to save. Police have come there and assaulted people. The authorities have proven that they will talk "with the language of force".

Where does all the hate in Russia come from? For example, Ludmila Ulitskaya and her pupils were attacked with green dye when they were attending a meeting of the human rights organisation Memorial. What is the source of such attitudes?

The people carrying out these attacks are trained puppies who were raised this way. Just like Hitler created his Hitlerjugend, Putin's youth has also been formed. They are free-will rapists and volunteers. The authorities disown them, saying "it is not us, they do what they want". Yet in fact, it is clear that the authorities created these people.

How can Europe help Russia? Political co-operation is frozen. Perhaps there is room left for cultural exchange…

I do not see any hope. Cultural encounters are initiated from above and only certain artists and people of culture are chosen to participate. The fact that

I could come here is an exception (the interview took place in Poland during the Miłosz literary festival in Kraków – editor's note). What I say has very little significance. At the same time, it seems that the situation cannot continue as it is. So, we live in a dilemma. You cannot live this way, but you cannot do anything about it.

In other words, you do not see any chance of things improving in Russia?

I cannot imagine what would have to happen for something to change. Even if Putin dies, will anything change? For sure, something will follow; a redistribution of power, perhaps. There are no people who would be trustworthy. Something should change, but not on a political level, not through elections.

Regardless, there is something that contradicts this bleakly pessimistic picture. There is a new type of development taking place in society. It is focused on voluntarism and is not political. People are united to help the most helpless parts of our society – sick children, for instance, or orphans, or the elderly who have nobody to help them. Another type of volunteer work is with disasters (fires, floods, etc.) and they show that they can be more effective than the state authorities. There is a volunteers' society called "Lisa Alert", which finds people who lose their way in the woods (for our police do not do it well). We never had that in Soviet times. This means that a new man is being formed. The fact that people want to do something together, they understand that they can achieve something and want to benefit specific areas and work in hotspots. What emerges is a different type of relationship between people, one that happens naturally, without the influence of Russian fatalism. The authorities have already learnt that this constitutes a threat, the fact that citizens who do not need them are forming. If the old Soviet man cannot live without the government, these people do not need it. I am happy about this process and it shows that perhaps there is a need to build a state from below.

That sounds like a western model…

I would say it is a normal model, one in which the government is accountable to those over whom it rules and who are the source of its power. There is no point in restructuring the system. Moreover, it is more interesting when someone manages to rescue a dozen kids without the support of the government than when someone goes out with a poster. It is a definite change when a Russian no longer complains and only cares about his or her own life. I was surprised by how egotistic the Soviet and post-Soviet people were. Now, a new type of citizen is forming in Russia. In my opinion, it is a miracle. NEE)

Translated by Agnieszka Pikulicka-Wilczewska

Olga Sedakova is a Russian poet and translator. She is the recipient of several literary prizes, including the Andrei Bely Prize, the European Prize in Poetry and the Solzhenitsyn Prize.

Masha Makarova is a Russian journalist currently based in Warsaw.

Is there a Transnistrian identity?

Interview with Nikolay Babilunga, a historian and dean of the Taras Shevchenko Transnistrian State University in Tiraspol. Interviewers: Tomasz Grzywaczewski and Tomasz Lachowski

TOMASZ GRZYWACZEWSKI AND TOMASZ LACHOWSKI: Do you see yourself as a Transnistrian, a Moldovan or just a citizen of one of those entities, without the need to define a nationality?

NIKOLAY BABILUNGA: For centuries, citizens from at least three nations lived on the territory of today's Transnistria: Moldovans, Russians and Ukrainians. Even so, none wanted to dominate the others, resulting in peaceful co-existence. Today, all three languages are officially recognised by the state and every citizen living on the left bank of the Dniester River (meaning Transnistria) can make their own choice as to who they are. The situation is similar with regards to religion. I certainly do not see any kind of potential threat to stability in Transnistria (bearing in mind relations with Moldova and Ukraine as well) based on religious issues.

I was born in Chişinău, the capital of Moldova. Soon after the completion of my studies, I decided to concentrate my research on the history of Moldova, with special reference to the Stalinist repressions that took place there. Prior to the Moldovan-Transnistrian War in the early 1990s, I moved to Tiraspol, a city that was known mostly for its industrial character during Soviet times. Although the Taras Shevchenko Transnistrian State University in Tiraspol was established in 1930, hardly anyone was researching the historical developments of this small strip of land between present day Moldova and Ukraine. This rather sad fact inspired me to create a special department within the structure of the university that focused on the history of Transnistria, as well as its neighbouring countries.

For obvious reasons, we could not leave Russia outside the scope of our academic interests. If you read history textbooks published in Transnistria, you can easily find everything you need: analyses of the 1917 Bolshevik Revolution, political repressions during Stalin's rule and post-war poverty and famine. Therefore, I disagree with those, predominantly in the West, who say that Transnistria is under the strong influence of Russian propaganda streaming directly from the Kremlin.

Given your position on the subject, it is important to emphasise that according to international law, Transnistria is still an integral part of Moldova. It seems the authorities in Tiraspol would like to erase that fact from their political agenda…

Western politicians and their experts often repeat this falsehood that Transnistria is a part of Moldova. It is not true. Historically, Moldova was located only on the right bank of the Dniester River, which was the natural border of its political influence in this part of Europe. What is more, I would emphasise the fact that some parts of Transnistria were located in the Polish-Lithuanian Commonwealth with the private estate of the Koniecpolski house, a Polish magnate family. Interestingly, the Koniecpolski family transferred their possessions to the Russian Empire. Thus, whilst there were Poles, Russians, Cossacks and Tatars living on Transnistrian soil, there were no Romanians or Moldovans. From my point of view, our Moldovans differ greatly from those living on the other side of the river. They are like distant cousins: – they may have the same roots, but their traditions are completely different.

Would you say that in the last 25 years Transnistria has succeeded in creating one political nation? Or is it still better to talk about three different nations living on the same territory?

Transnistria is undoubtedly one nation. However, it consists of three different ethnicities. Furthermore, we cannot forget about the other nationalities whose homeland is in Transnistria: the Gagauz, Bulgarians, Jews and Poles. The latter can be found mostly in the north, in a neighbourhood of the city of Rashkovo. A small nearby village, Sloboda Rashkovo, is a typical Polish settlement. If you were to ask the residents what nationality they are, they would almost certainly reply: "Polish". Even so, I do not believe that the will to cultivate a Polish tradition is in any way a threat to our small republic.

Recently, a group of anthropologists and an ethnologist from the Russian Academy of Sciences conducted a research project focusing on national identity in three ethnicities: Moldovan, Gagauzian and Transnistrian. According to the results, our republic's identity is based on a key geographical factor, the Dniester River, which forms not only our administrative and political boundary, but also a mental one. In Moldova, the definition of identity was always based on ethnic divisions. Some Moldovans feel intrinsically Romanian whilst others feel Moldovan. In Transnistria, this ethnic divide was never important. Today, nearly 50 per cent of the population living on the left bank declare their identity to be "Transnistrian", while in Moldova, only 30 per cent consider themselves to be Moldovan. Bearing this in mind, which

Photo by Agnieszka Pikulicka-Wilczewska

A beauty salon in Tiraspol adorned by a sign glorifying victory in the Great Patriotic War. "I would not call 'Russification' our problem, we are part of a world that is ruled by Moscow," says Nikolay Babilunga, a historian based in Transnistria.

country do you think is more artificial, Moldova or Transnistria? For people living in Tiraspol, as well as other Transnistrian cities like Rybnitsa or Dubossary, a connection to a political structure is more important than one based on blood ties with a particular nation. I would say that sounds more like a modern approach to citizenship, does it not?

How would you respond to Moldova's accusations regarding a policy of discrimination, especially based on language, conducted by the Transnistrian authorities?

This issue is based on the false assumption that the denationalisation of Moldovans living on the left bank is strictly a political problem. The aim of such pressure is to improve Moldova's standing in the eyes of western leaders. On the other hand, it is true that in most

schools, you would find more textbooks printed in the Russian Federation and written in Russian than in Moldovan. However, this does not mean that there is a policy of discrimination against Moldovans residing in Transnistria.

The education system in Transnistria and the prevalence of Russian books confirm the fact that Soviet and Russian symbols dominate the public sphere. These include not just the hammer and sickle or the monuments of Lenin seen in city squares, but also a recurring commemoration of the heroes of the Great Patriotic War and those fighting for the glory of the Tsar. Could such a level of Russification be a threat to the emerging Transnistrian identity that you have just outlined?

Regarding the question of Russian textbooks, I do not see any kind of Muscovite supremacy in our school curriculum. Instead, I would say that there is a quantitative, not qualitative, predomination. In Transnistria there are Ukrainian, Moldovan, Bulgarian and even Polish schools. Unfortunately we lack valuable manuals written in these languages. Therefore, there is an urgent need to address this issue. At the same time, I disagree that Russian textbooks are being promoted by the Transnistrian authorities. As an academic involved in the preparation of such books for students, I try to compare and analyse what this process looks like in other countries, particularly with regards to a school history course that is taught in Russia and other post-Soviet states. Sometimes I get the feeling that these books are written to prove a point, one primarily concocted by politicians.

Once I received a high school textbook titled *The history of crisis in Russia*. After reading it, a student could easily have an impression that the fate of such a geographically large and politically strong state as Russia, from the Empire through to today's Federation, was just a history of failures and geopolitical mistakes. The tendency to write books in this way was particularly prevalent in the Russian Federation in the early 1990s, just after the dissolution of the Soviet Union. It seems that someone was trying to shape the Russian youth in order to weaken the country itself.

Now, to address the alleged Russification. Forgive me, but it makes me laugh. The last public opinion poll conducted in Transnistria demonstrated very clearly that around 95 per cent of respondents want to have some kind of connection with Russia. In 2006 a referendum that achieved polling numbers of 97 per cent led to a move towards full independence and, subsequently, integration with the Russian Federation. The same situation is taking place today, especially after Crimea joined Russia. Therefore, I would not call "Russification" our problem. We are part of a world that is ruled by Moscow. The question remains whether countries like Ukraine and Moldova, which are more politically oriented towards the West these days, could ever really succeed in excoriating everything that associates them with Russia.

You mentioned the involvement of a third state in the political affairs of a country. As a result of the armed conflict in Ukraine, two parallel narratives have appeared. On the one side was the idea of a liberal democracy symbolised by the European Union, whilst on the other was the *Russkiy mir* (Russian World) governed by the Kremlin. Even though Moldova is definitely not a stable country, the last election resulted in small gains for the pro-European factions. In your opinion, does this mean that Transnistria is being forced to choose Moscow?

I try to avoid referring to the Ukrainian crisis as a spontaneous civic protest that took place in Kyiv. What I will say is that a conflict in Ukraine was created and is being prolonged by people who are not taking care of ordinary Ukrainian citizens. Of course, you can use some carrots (such as the pro-EU attempts at reform), but at the same time you also need to find a stick. The upsurge in nationalism occurring in Ukraine at the moment, as epitomised by parties like "Pravyy Sector" or "Svoboda", was initially very useful for the post-Maidan authorities in order to highlight their differences with Russia. However, the presence of such factions in Ukraine's political landscape has generated political chaos and may turn out to be very dangerous, not just for Petro Poroshenko and Volodymyr Groysman (Ukraine's president and prime minister respectively), but also for the common people.

Western countries are well-known for their destabilisation policies in various parts of the world. Ukraine just happened to be next on the list. The massive immigration crisis and the waves of refugees coming from the Middle East and North Africa serve as proof of the irresponsibility of these policies. However, there is a burning need to safeguard states against the most severe nationalist infection: Nazism (the reason why the situation in Ukraine is so delicate). In Transnistria, we understand that although the republic is culturally Russian, there is no point in completely rejecting the achievements and legacy of the western world.

How would you assess the idea of reintegrating Transnistria into Moldova, assuming Transnistria received broad autonomy? What parameters would this potential federation need in order to protect Transnistria's interests?

To answer this question I will refer back to the late 1980s and the agony of the *perestroika* movement invented by Mikhail Gorbachev. In the Moldavian Soviet Socialist Republic, much like in other republics within the Soviet Union, "restructuring" meant the revival of a wave of nationalism, Romanian in this particular case. Firstly, this resulted in legal efforts to establish Romanian as the only official state language. Secondly, all non-Romanian citizens were discriminated against. This maltreatment was based on their ethnic origin, so it was not only Slavs (Russians or Ukrainians) who were persecuted, but also all remaining minorities, including Jews. Therefore, at the beginning of the 1990s, the Transnistrian population was forced to protect its own interests. Contrary to the narrative formed and promoted by Chișinău, we did not think about full independence or sovereignty of a separatist regime.

During the term of President Mircea Snegur Moldova imposed Romanian national symbols on Transnistria. What is more, the 1991 Moldovan Declaration of Independence left no space for any minorities or autonomous regions that did not fit with the central authorities' vision of a future Moldova. This situation was repeated in Transnistria, Gagauzia and Bukovina. Do we really need to form one state with Moldova? Nationalist tendencies, strengthened by the idea of joining Romania, are still very strong there and so are interpreted as a threat to the peaceful existence of the Transnistrian state.

The last two or three years have been quite turbulent for post-Soviet republics. There is an ongoing armed conflict in eastern Ukraine, there were some clashes on the South Ossetia border in late summer 2015 and intense fighting broke out in Nagorno-Karabakh in April 2016. Are people in Tiraspol still worried about the possibility of an escalation of the Russian-Ukrainian war that could spill over to Transnistria? In July 2015 Yevgeny Shevchuk, Transnistria's "president", even ordered a mobilisation of troops.

Let me be clear: Transnistria does not want to attack anyone. Nevertheless, all the events that are unfolding behind our eastern border, especially in Odesa, do not fill us with much optimism. Even so, this does not mean that our small republic would start a war with Ukraine. Personally, I am worried about the behaviour of Mikheil Saakashvili, the current Governor of Ukraine's Odesa Oblast. He lost almost everything in the eyes of his compatriots in Georgia. Trying to uphold his strong anti-Russian position, he might do something stupid. For example, if Saakashvili orders his troops to shoot at the Russian peacekeepers staying in Transnistria, the Kremlin would definitely react.

In your view, is a war in this part of Europe possible? Would Putin decide to use his troops again in order to make his notion of *Novorossiya* a reality?

I truly hope that world leaders are not heading towards bloodshed. On the other hand, I am sure that for the past 25 years the people living on the left bank of the Dniester River have been aware of its geopolitical situation, freedom and (limited, but tangible) independence. With the help of the Russian peacekeepers, we are ready to protect our values. Today we discussed the issue of Transnistrian identity a lot. This will be invoked as our first achievement of the last 25 years. Self-awareness, as well as a distinct national interest and security, are our second. NEE)

Nikolay Babilunga is a historian based in Transnistria, a quasi-state within the territory of Moldova. He is the dean of and a professor at the Taras Shevchenko Transnistrian State University in Tiraspol, researching historical justifications for the existence of a separate Transnistrian nation and its right to self-determination. He was a dissident during Soviet times.

Tomasz Grzywaczewski is a lawyer and journalist. He is a PhD candidate at the department of international law and international relations at the University of Łódź (Poland). He is editor-in-chief of the magazine *Koncept – Gazeta Akademicka*.

Tomasz Lachowski is a lawyer and journalist. He holds a PhD in international law and is a researcher at the department of international law and international relations at the University of Łódź (Poland) and editor-in-chief of the magazine *Obserwator Międzynarodowy*.

A shell-shocked city: two years on

WOJCIECH KOŹMIC

In a tiny asphalt alley, located not far from the airport in Donetsk, it is easy to spot traces of the explosions from the infamous Grad shelling. The houses located along the street near the airport have either been destroyed or severely damaged. There are virtually no people in the area. The atmosphere of apparent calmness, so discernible in the city centre, is also absent. After all, only a dozen or so kilometres separate these two places. What then differentiates the tidy central streets of Donetsk to the suburbs of the city, which used to be home to a million inhabitants?

A lake located in central Donetsk is divided by a long pedestrian bridge. At the entrance, between the trees, one can see a rope park. A small tent tempts passers-by with sweet candy floss. However, the main attractions prepared for the celebrations on May 9th are located a few hundred meters away. Concerts dedicated to the anniversary of Victory Day are taking place there and are one of the main events around which the day-long celebrations are centred. The crowd reacts with more enthusiasm when a Russian band comes on stage. A few flags are fluttering, including Russian ones. Everyone is chanting the catchy word: "Novorossiya, Novorossiya!" Police with dogs and military police are closely watching the scene.

Political souvenirs

In actual fact, the real festival is taking place in a nearby park, with a variety of amusement rides and a shooting range. Apart from standard targets at the shooting range, one can also shoot the faces of Ukrainian politicians: President Petro Poroshenko and the former Prime Minister Arseniy Yatsenyuk.

In this context, it is worth looking back to the days of EuroMaidan for a moment. At that time, the main political opponents of the Maidan community were printed on toilet paper and doormats. One could spend money on a "political souvenir" and take out their anger and other emotions on said product. Initially, Yanukovych was the most popular enemy, but later, Vladimir Putin undisputedly took over this mantle.

The war in Donbas widened the assortment of souvenirs and introduced the idea of shooting at targets with the face of the Russian president. Thus, the innovative targets in Donetsk are not an entirely new idea. Although Yatsenyuk is no longer Ukraine's prime minister, for those wanting to shoot at him it does not seem to matter. For the inhabitants of the separatist Donetsk People's Republic (DNR), the target represents the enemy, the other, someone who contributed to the war in Donbas, which led to the death of many people.

At the beginning of May 2016 Donetsk prepared two celebrations. May 9th is the day of huge celebrations commemorating the victory of the Soviet Union in the Second World War, 71 years ago. Beyond that, May 11th is the day the DNR celebrated the second anniversary of its foundation, although practically no country has recognised its existence. While the May 9th celebrations focused more on the military, the second holiday became a demonstration of the Donbas people. The region's strength and its differences from Ukraine are manifested by the masses.

The inhabitants of various districts in Donetsk march in front of a tribune decorated with the colours of the republic. Representatives of the republic's cities and trade unions, students, artists and teenagers all march together. Decorated car carriers follow. Even a tractor and a combine harvester appear. For over two hours, Alexander Zakharchenko, the DNR's leader, has been greeting the participants from a tribune decorated with the colours of the republic.

Life is easier

A few dozen metres away, I speak with volunteers from South Ossetia (a Georgian territory under Russian control after the 2008 Russia-Georgia War – editor's note), who draw attention because of their characteristic flags. They are some of the many foreigners who arrived in Donbas at the beginning of the war. Some of them have already returned to their homes, some stayed and kept fighting. People eagerly take photographs with them. "Have you been here from the beginning?" I ask one of the Ossetian volunteers.

"Yes, from the start, and we do not know how long we will stay," he responds. There is no shadow of a doubt when it comes to their intentions regarding their participation in the conflict. They recall their own fight against Georgians. For them, the war in Donbas is similar.

Not only are Ossetian volunteers involved in the support of separatist forces since the beginning of the war, one of the few official delegations taking part in the DNR celebrations came from South Ossetia. A young man joins our conversation. He comes from Donetsk and is interested in history. However, we talk mainly about his current life in Donetsk.

"Psychologically, life is easier for us now," he says calmly. Although he acknowledges that there are huge problems with finding work, one feels that the first aspect is more important to him. The chance to speak Russian and participate in the celebrations, which are now viewed negatively in Ukraine, clearly matter to him. Economic factors are consigned to the background. I hear similar sentiments throughout my time in Donetsk. People who are critical of Ukraine often highlight the importance of such elements, which are crucial for shaping their nascent identity.

When "Grad" falls from the sky

An imaginary border dividing Donetsk between those parts experiencing a relatively calm existence during the conflict and those where the war is still highly visible is represented by the train station building. A number of the station's windows have been damaged and are covered by wooden planks. However, if one goes further to the north, the images get worse. Here, more houses show traces of fighting, while some buildings have been completely destroyed. It is a result of the battles for Donetsk airport and the close proximity of the front, which is based in the suburbs of the city. Conversations with people have a very different character here. No one talks about victory, but rather about the tragedies the people have experienced. An older couple invite me into their house. In front of the

> Conversations with people in the suburbs of Donetsk are very different. No one talks about victory, but rather about the tragedies that the people have experienced.

house, in a narrow asphalt alley, one can see regularly spaced holes caused by Grad shells, probably caused by the Ukrainian side.

They point to various places marked by the shelling. Their home has suffered as well. Half-jokingly, I say that they have become specialists in artillery. "I am an artillerist myself and I knew exactly what fell here", the man replies with a firm voice. "There is standing water in our house and for a year and a half, we have lived without electricity", the woman adds nervously. "And adding to all that, the looting of the houses that have been left behind is also taking place. The looters stole everything from our son's house." The couple talk about the challenge of securing their possessions and the inequities of war.

It is clear that the couple are fighting their own private war, one that has not ended with the cessation of military operations in the area. In addition, they do not see evil only on one side. Evil surrounds them in every way. As someone shot, someone else stole, while no one wants to help them rebuild their house. They stayed here only because they had nowhere else to go. Despite this, they will not leave the house at the mercy of looters.

I have a similar conversation not far from the couple's home, close to the totally destroyed airport in Donetsk. However, the people I speak with here put more emphasis on the victims. They calmly point at places where their neighbours died.

"Right here," around 15 metres separate us from the first death. "There, behind the street," not more than 30 metres. One feels that their most cherished dream is peace and quiet. A woman, who serves me tea, says with sorrow: "I work at the rail station. I have not yet received my salary for February (we speak in the first half of May – author's note). I mean that Ukraine stopped paying our salaries and the DNR has not yet begun to pay them. I will never be able to repair my house with the money I receive."

Out of curiosity, she asks me who is staying on the frontlines on the Ukrainian side. Are they the well-known Ukrainian "penal battalions" (a term used by the separatist side), whose presence is frequently highlighted by the separatist and Russian media? Although it is clear that she disdains the frontline presence of these troops, she talks about the DNR soldiers in the third person. It is clear that she does not fully identify with them, although theoretically, they defend her from the Ukrainian army, including the malevolent nationalist divisions. The way she speaks and the words she chooses clearly indicate that she is trying to distance herself from the conflict as much as possible. She does not hide the fact that she would like to see her future, and the future of Donetsk, under any rule which would guarantee a relatively peaceful life. It can be Ukraine or the DNR, as long as they let people live a calm life.

A grey mess

The exhaustion with the conflict and the private issues of those affected totally alter the hierarchy of values. Any attachment to a state entity is invisible. There is, at most, a regional identity. Above all though, is the apparent will to survive this turmoil. The fervent opponents of the Donbas inhabitants' mentality and the actions of the region's political elite could in this moment ask: was the hierarchy here ever any different?

> Any attachment to a state entity is invisible. There is, at most, a regional identity.

Are there people who support Ukraine in the Donetsk People's Republic? There are, but it is not easy to find them. At the same time, it is hardly an open secret. Among networks of families and friends, such knowledge is common.

I slowly gain the trust of my interlocutor, who gradually begins to tell me about her Donetsk, where she now feels like she is in a prison. She is terrified by what has happened to her city and the people with whom she must work and talk. She does not accept their views or the hatred of Ukraine which nested deep in the minds of many people. "How many people who support Ukraine still live in Donetsk?" I ask.

She begins her long story: "Maybe it is as much as ten per cent. I think that a similar number strongly support the DNR, but the rest are a grey mass which will adapt. For them, it is all the same. The older generation tends to trust Zakharchenko; their lives have finally changed for the better. They receive pensions from both the DNR and from Ukraine. However, others do not trust or respect him … I went into a shop with my husband recently and there were blue and yellow hats. I saw two young girls trying them on in front of a mirror, one of them, the yellow one, and the other, the blue one. They laughed and quickly put them back. You know, it takes courage to do something like that these days. It could land you in prison." NEE

Translated by Agnieszka Pikulicka-Wilczewska

Wojciech Koźmic is a Polish civil society activist and *New Eastern Europe*'s photo-reporter. You can see more photos from the May 11th 2016 celebrations in Donetsk on our web site at: www.neweasterneurope.eu.

"I Love the DNR (Donetsk People's Republic)".

The people in the DNR show signs of exhaustion with the conflict. What they want most is to be left to live a relatively peaceful life, it does not matter if it is in Ukraine or the DNR.

At the beginning of May Donetsk prepares two celebrations. May 9th commemorates the victory of the Soviet Union in the Second World War. May 11th is the day the DNR celebrates the anniversary of its founding, although practically no country has recognised its existence.

Photo by Wojciech Koźmic

A zone of limited freedom

The last time I came to Luhansk was in October 2014. It was a month after the Ukrainian offensive had been halted for the first time. Two years later, I returned to find that the Luhansk of 2014 no longer exists. What remains is an almost empty city, whose authorities are desperately trying to prove that life is better here than ever before.

Luhansk looks lazy and empty. Most of its inhabitants have not come back after the heavy fighting that took place in and around the city in 2014 as there is little opportunity for a normal life anymore. It is better to stay in Russia, other parts of Ukraine or wherever one went in 2014. Luhansk appears to be the opposite of Donetsk, where signs of life exist, including more people, cars on the streets and new or re-opened restaurants. On the near-empty streets of Luhansk life is slow as there is no reason to rush. Finding work is not easy either. As a result, shops tend to sell only basic goods.

Private companies offer services to get money from Ukrainian bank accounts that do not work in the territories controlled by the separatists. Tensions are rare because the frontline, located about 15 kilometres from the city, is almost quiet. Separatists from the so-called Luhansk People's Republic (LNR) are more involved in politics than fighting. Their primary concerns are food prices, water sources, the building of the republic and the elimination of rivals.

Leaving hell

The last time I came to Luhansk was in October 2014. It was a month after the Ukrainian offensive had been halted for the first time. The city was surrounded by pro-government forces, some of whom had already reached the northern parts of Crimea. Everybody thought that Luhansk was just days away from being retaken from separatist control. However, the pro-government forces had lost the battle of Ilovaysk (around 50 kilometres from Donetsk) and Russian tanks appeared in Novoazovsk (more than 40 kilometres from main port of Mariupol). In the Luhansk region, Ukrainian soldiers were ordered to withdraw over the river Donets, where they remain to this day.

In 2014 the city began to show traces of the fighting. The most obvious signs were destroyed buildings, many of which were riddled with shrapnel. The worst damage was in the suburbs and outside the city. Outside Luhansk it was sometimes hard to figure out where a building had once stood. The infrastructure in the city centre was also not immune to shelling. Tap water was available only in certain areas and residents were forced to queue in front of the fire brigade building for water, patiently waiting for a chance to fill up their buckets and go home. The same applied to electricity. There was no light in the streets and traffic lights were turned off. Curfew in the city would start at 9pm, but even as early as 5pm it was hard to see anybody on the dark and empty streets. Along the main street, called Radianska, one could see the dim light of candle flames emanating from people's homes.

> The worst damage to Luhansk was in the suburbs and outside the city. Out there, it was sometimes hard to figure out where a building had once stood.

As the hotels did not have either electricity or water, I decided to find a flat. Landlords gave me a choice: a flat with electricity or one with water. For me, it was a no brainer; I needed electricity since I had to send news reports to different newspapers and media outlets. As a matter of fact, in Ukraine internet connections are often better than phone lines, so it was not particularly surprising when I located a fast connection. By opting for electricity, I had no choice but to queue for water with my buckets every day.

Most of the city's residents had fled by the summer of 2014, when the worst of the fighting took place. All the buildings at the regional airport were totally destroyed by September 2014 and all that remained were its ruins. Unlike at Donetsk airport, there was no brave stand taken to defend the territory, just a short, dramatic battle. Once the fighting had finished, locals looking for easy money looted kilos of scrap metal. In 2014 Luhansk, which was never an especially well-developed city or region to begin with, became a ghost town.

Lost in the supermarket

Upon returning to the city two years later, I learnt that the Luhansk of 2014 no longer exists. The self-proclaimed authorities are doing everything they can to demonstrate to those that remain that they made the right choice by supporting (or at least not opposing) the separatists. Shops are not as empty as before. Products are usually imported from Russia or come from elsewhere in the region. Sometimes, they are produced in Belarus, although it is rare to find European products from other countries. Unlike in Donetsk, goods made in Ukraine are especially hard to find. Road checkpoints, where one can cross the unofficial border between the territories controlled by the separatists and those which are controlled by Kyiv, are mostly located in the Donetsk region. Thus, transporting goods to Luhansk increases the price of already expensive products.

To maintain control over prices, the self-proclaimed authorities decided to monitor them in supermarkets and bazars every week. During meetings between "government" ministers, reports about prices, the production of goods and other problems in the "republic" are read. The self-proclaimed head of the LNR, Ihor Plotnitsky, tries to act like Vladimir Putin: tough, serious and fearsome. Participating ministers sit with grumpy faces and await their turn to report about the current situation. If Plotnistky does not like what he hears, he becomes angry and shouts. This is all done in the presence of the local media.

"Do I understand you correctly when you say that we cannot make prices for water lower?" Plotnitsky asks the acting minister for economic development and trade, Elena Kostenko. "How come tap water is more expensive, and then they bottle it and pretend that we have mineral water?" he asks ironically. Kostenko does not answer and Plotnisky continues to reprimand other ministers.

Alevtina is the head of the price monitoring group. She is around fifty and not happy that journalists are here. She does not want to talk to the cameras because she sometimes travels to the territories controlled by Kyiv. Any appearance in the media could cause her problems because she officially works for the separatists.

Alvetina takes us to a supermarket which used to belong to the ATB chain of markets and is now called the People's ("nationalised") supermarket. "Here, you cannot shoot pictures or video, but you can see how we work. If you want to take pictures, you need special permission from the supermarket's security office," she says. In the LNR, almost every institution has its own security service. As Alvetina explained to me, the self-proclaimed authorities are really cautious about showing products and prices to the public. "It could be used against us by the other side," she says. The phrase "the other side" clearly refers to Ukraine. "How can they use it?" I ask a bit confused. She does not offer an explanation.

Alevtina and her team walk around the supermarket, checking the prices of basic products such as water, flour, grain, milk, sugar, salt, meat and others. This practice is designed to ensure that these products do not cost more than the designated "government" prices. For example, a kilogram of chicken cannot cost more than 116 roubles (around 1.80 US dollars). "We are already seeing prices that are between 90–111 roubles. The market is saturated so prices are decreasing," she says.

However, she also notes that prices for meat are still too high. This is particularly notable with beef, which is very limited in the territories controlled by the separatists. "There are many shops which are well-stocked so they are trying to compete with each other," argues Alevtina. "I think that in the republic, we have products for every customer."

The less you know

The social situation is becoming more stable but there is still no clear idea what will really happen to the territories controlled by the separatists. Will they become independent, join Russia or go back to Ukraine? Alevtina is sure that the third of these options is best: "I think it is no secret. It is a common view. We just want some concessions," she says. In her opinion, granting autonomy, like in Crimea (before the annexation), would be enough to end the conflict. Standing next to Alevtina is a journalist from the local media, staring blankly at the floor. She probably decided that it would be better not to talk about this subject at all. In Luhansk, I have already heard the expression, "the less you know, the longer you live" (or in a soft version "sleep") quite a few times.

> The social situation is becoming more stable in Luhansk, but there is still no idea what will really happen to the territories controlled by the separatists.

However, the sleepy and lazy atmosphere here can be misleading. Since the onset, the fight for power in the LNR has been brutal. Charismatic and undisciplined commanders were assassinated, as was the case with the leader of the "Ghost" battalion, Oleksandr Mozgovy. Others, like Mykola Kozitsyn, lost their influence. Only Plotnisky remains (though an assassination attempt was made in early August 2016). The local media are important as they are the local authorities' main propaganda tool. Residents can watch local TV via broadcast television, along with other Russian TV channels.

The main local station focuses on showing the successes of the "young republic" and its leader. In almost every programme, Plotnisky appears as a good shepherd who takes care of his flock. The head of the republic opens a school after its restoration, forces prices to be lowered and visits an exhibition put on by local artists. Plotnisky is everywhere and the local media make sure you do not forget it.

In between news broadcasts, old Soviet movies or new, tasteless Russian series are shown, where everything is happening in an IKEA-style flat, which the poor citizens of Luhansk cannot even begin to dream about. The dream of a swanky life in Russia was one of the reasons why some of the residents of Donbas decided to support the Russian-backed separatist movement two years ago. They truly believed that it would be the first step to joining Russia, just as Crimea did. They hoped that their lives would improve to the standard shown on Russian TV.

However, these series depict life in Moscow and St Petersburg, where only a small number of citizens are similarly wealthy. From this perspective, Russia looks much more attractive than it really is. On other hand, the old movies hark back to the "great times", when the Soviet Union was one of the main actors in the global system. People still feel a great sense of pride about that period of history and it is this that the separatists use in their propaganda: Soviet nostalgia, welfare and the appeal of the highlife lived by Moscow's upper middle class.

Slavs unite!

Another element of the propaganda machine is the Russian Orthodox Church, which was actively working with the rebels right from the start. During my recent stay I attended a discussion with students called "What is the Russian civilisation?", which was led by Orthodox priests. I myself have been searching for an answer to this question since the beginning of the war. I still could not find out around which values and identities the "republics" mobilised support, especially after they began to understand that Russia was not going to annex them.

After two years of propaganda and social engineering it seems that the best answer the authorities could come up with is to be found in silly movies which suggest that everything is a masonic plot aimed to destroy the Slavic identity and make Slavs the slaves

> Another element of the propaganda machine is the Russian Orthodox Church, which was actively working with the rebels from the beginning.

of the West. To counter this threat, they should unite under Russia's supremacy and stand up for their rights.

"All these Maidans took place because Ukrainians want to clean toilets in Europe," says Vitaly Darensky, a writer from Luhansk, during the discussion. "It makes no difference what passport you have, it is what is in your soul that counts," adds Mykola Shkodyn, a priest. According to his words, what really counts is whether or not the identity residing in one's soul is Russian

Still hoping to find an answer for reasons to support the separatists, I decided to meet with a local intellectual. We meet in a park which is in the city centre; nobody is sitting near us. She is well-known here and was popular among Ukrainian artists before war. When she decided to stand on the side of the rebels from Luhansk, it surprised many people. Most of her friends were forced to leave the city because of their pro-Ukrainian views. Yet, she stayed. I expected to see her full of passion and talking like Lenin. Instead, she seemed scared and chose every word very carefully. She was wary and not confident. She told me that the LNR is a "zone of freedom". When asked, she could not explain to me what that meant. I press her, trying to get an answer.

"I know that many strange things are still happening here, but I cannot say what in an interview, especially with foreign media," she finally admits, ending our conversation. NEE)

Paweł Pieniążek is a Polish journalist, specialising in Eastern Europe. He regularly contributes to the Polish daily *Dziennik Opinii* and *New Eastern Europe*. He is the author of the book *Greetings from Novorossiya*, which was published in Poland.

How much Königsberg is in Kaliningrad?

PAULINA SIEGIEŃ

The last two years have seen a real boom when it comes to discovering the identity of Königsberg in Kaliningrad. There are numerous associations, initiatives, individuals and groups who have set out to follow the trail of the city and the region's pre-war past, with increased interest in Kaliningrad's history, memory and local identity.

For lovers of Eastern Prussia history in the early 1990s, the case of Kaliningrad was like a Kinder Egg: everyone wanted to break it open and find out what was inside. Indeed, the post-war fate of Königsberg stimulated the curiosity of historians, anthropologists and journalists alike. First *perestroika*, and later the collapse of the Soviet Union, opened the Kaliningrad Oblast and their hunger for knowledge could be satisfied. This is the reason why many travel reports about Kaliningrad originate from the 1990s.

This esteemed collection includes the writings of Anne Applebaum, who had gone on a journey along the former western border of the Soviet Union and in doing so, reached the Kaliningrad Oblast. Her reporting paints an image of a disoriented society, orphaned by the USSR and in search of a new identity. It was at this point, Applebaum noted, that the pre-war Prussian history of the city and the region became a reference point in the search to discover Kaliningraders' identity.

Two cities, two histories

Today, even a short visit to Kaliningrad is enough to convince one that the city's Germanic past plays a crucial role in shaping the city's narrative identity. At the same time, it is difficult to disagree with the *Neue Zurchner Zeitung* reporter Judith Leister, who believes that Kaliningrad and Königsberg are two separate entities which function in parallel. In a similar way, Małgorzata Omilanowska, a Gdańsk-based art historian and former Polish minister of culture, argues that Kaliningrad is an example of a complete break in historical and cultural continuity. Indeed, this city does not have one coherent story to present, unlike, Gdańsk.

Kaliningrad's pre-war history and culture were erased during Soviet times, both literally and figuratively. The material traces of Königsberg were demolished and a discussion of the city's German past was restricted. The iconic symbol of this Soviet policy towards the capital of former Eastern Prussia was the demolition of the Royal Castle in 1968. Old photographs show the remaining fragments, which would have allowed for a reconstruction of the old building. Sadly, ideology obliterated it into the annals of history.

> Kaliningrad's pre-war history and culture were erased in Soviet times, literally and figuratively.

The year 2005 was a key year in the process of resurrecting the city's pre-war memory, as this was the year that the city organised festivities to celebrate its 750th birthday. The host of the celebrations was none other than Vladimir Putin. For the local residents and the intellectual elite, the celebrations illustrated that the process of rebuilding the city's identity was enabling it to go back to its roots and that its history started in 1255, not 1946. During the celebrations, Putin was presented with a mock-up of the Royal Castle and asked to express his opinion about its reconstruction. The Russian president not only liked the idea but also promised to assign funding from the federal budget to aid the project.

Putin's special treatment towards Kaliningrad was explained by the fact that his wife at the time, Lyudmila, was born there. However, a more convincing explanation is that Putin, who was keener to maintain good relations with the West in the early years of his presidency, was convinced that due to its history and location, Kaliningrad could play a special role in Russia's rapprochement with the West. This was interpreted not only as a symbolic but also strategic gesture, since the anniversary celebrations were attended by high-level guests such as then German Chancellor Gerhard Schroeder and France's then president, Jacques Chirac. Notably, the presidents of neighbouring Poland and Lithuania were not invited, which shows that Putin's goal was not to build good neighbourly relations but begin the

References to history and the pre-war aesthetics are exploited by local businesses in Kaliningrad. A good example is the network of bakeries and cafés called Königsbäcker.

western pivot for Russia's foreign policy. As a matter of fact, in the first term of Putin's presidency, the Kaliningrad Oblast was seen as an experimental platform for Russia-EU relations. Therefore, Königsberg's 750th anniversary celebrations did not impede the organisation of the 60th anniversary celebrations of the Kaliningrad Oblast, held in 2006. Crucially, this double narrative has continued to exist up until the present day.

Rediscovering Königsberg

The last two years have seen a real boom when it comes to discovering the identity of Königsberg in Kaliningrad. There are numerous associations, initiatives, individuals and groups who have set out to follow the trail of the city and the region's pre-war past. Increased interest in Kaliningrad's history, memory and local identity is also one of the key outcomes of the 2012 Law on Small Border Traffic, which simplified border crossing rules for those Kaliningrad residents who wanted to visit border areas in Poland, including the city of Gdańsk, and vice versa. The case of Gdańsk and its experience building a post-war urban narrative differently to Soviet Kaliningrad stresses its historical continuity. It became an inspiration for the discussions about re-building Kaliningrad's historical centre. Gdańsk is not just a destination for ordinary Kaliningrad residents, who admire its reconstructed old town, but also for the city's authorities, who have been hosted there many times. These experiences enabled them to see that history, just like culture and architecture, can turn a city into an interesting tourist destination.

The construction of the empty House of Soviets dominates the site of what is considered Kaliningrad's historical centre. This building was one of the largest construction projects in the Soviet Union and, ironically, ended up suffering the same fate. The collapse of the Soviet Union halted the building's completion. The unfinished structure, which the residents used to call "Monster", has nonetheless become a city landmark, seen by many as a symbol of Kaliningrad. An urban legend holds that the sad fate of the building is Prussia's revenge for the destruction of the Royal Castle which once sat slightly further to the west in the same square.

> In 2013 Kaliningrad set up an urban planning bureau called the Heart of the City to popularise the idea of building a historical centre.

For years, only the wind entered the empty construction site of the House of Soviets, as nobody knew how to make use of the area (with the exception of those who used it as an open-air market). In 2013 the Kaliningrad authorities decided to finally put a stop to the impasse. An urban planning bureau called the Heart of the City was set up. It was given the task of popularising the idea of building a historical centre, undertaking social consultations and, above all, organising requests for urban and architectural proposals. In the official statement on the Heart of the City website, one can read about the need "to bring back the historical area of Königsberg to [Kaliningrad's] urban setting (...) as well as creating an individual, architectonic image of a 'place' – a cultural identification, that will become a mark of today's Kaliningrad, which is a part of the global world, the Baltic Sea region and Russia at the same time".

To fulfil these obligations the Heart of the City announced two calls for proposals, one of them directed at the reconstruction of the Royal Castle. Upon receiving numerous submissions, the jury announced that the winning project was created by Anton Sagal. Sagal is a Russian architect working in Milan. His proposal was for a modern construction, where a few of elements resembled the historical shape of the castle. However, in the online vote, run by popular local website www.newkaliningrad.ru, it was Arthur Sarnits' project that won. Using documents that had been collected over the years, Sarnits and his team prepared a detailed visualisation of the Royal Castle and its surroundings, which were to be presented in their original shape. However, his project caused a lot of controversy among experts, mainly because of its directness. Conversely, and not entirely surprisingly, the city authorities liked it. Sarnits is a close friend of Nikolay Tsukanov, the governor of Kaliningrad oblast at the time. By the end of July 2016 Tsukanov was dismissed and replaced by Evgeniy Zinichev – a general of the Federal Security Service (FSB). As of the writing of this article, his position on the castle's reconstruction is unknown.

Path to destruction

In the spring of 2016 the deputy prime minister of the Kaliningrad government, Garri Goldman, announced in interviews with the Kaliningrad media that by 2018, the year that Russia would be hosting the FIFA World Cup, the western wing of the castle, based on Sarnits' project, would be completed. However, he did not know whose design the construction of the remainder would be based on.

By ignoring the results of the Heart of the City competition and sacking the previous director of the Heart of the City organisation, the city authorities generated significant anger among residents, who viewed this behaviour as a simple path to undoing the earlier efforts of the Heart of the City team and its first director, Alexander Popadin. In addition, external observers, such as Polish professor Jerzy Gąssowski, have highlighted the danger of the castle's foundations being destroyed by unprofessional archaeological work.

Unsurprisingly, Kaliningrad residents are already making some dark predictions. Many believe that once the World Cup is over and the walls of the castle's west wing are up, there will be no money or investment left to finish the job. Consequently, the castle will become a *долгострой*, the Russian name for building projects whose construction suffers endless delays. The castle will then share the same sad fate as its neighbour, the House of Soviets. Others fear that the successful completion of the construction mean that it will not become the headquarters of a cultural institution, but yet another commercial object, such as a shopping mall.

Their fears are reinforced by decisions such as that to build a housing estate next to the House of Soviets, which is adjacent to where the Castle is planned. The Heart of the City initiative, which was welcomed by the Kaliningrad public with great interest and hope, seems to have become discredited.

As part of this whole discussion, it is worth bringing up one argument that is advocated by those who admire the city's Prussian past but who nonetheless oppose the castle's reconstruction. They point out that in the city of Kaliningrad and throughout the whole oblast, there are many objects of great historical, cultural and architectural value which are falling into ruin. The process of bringing back Königsberg heritage to the urban space of Kaliningrad should not, as they argue, ignore these places at the expense of the castle. Understandably, it is easier to find an investor willing to build a replica than one who will back the reconstruction of pre-war buildings. The best example of this is the near-collapse of the "Kreuz-Apotheke": it was impossible to find a buyer who would be willing to purchase it, even for a single, symbolic rouble, as the proposal submission criteria required that the buyer would have to reconstruct the ruined building.

From Kaliningrad to Königbserg

Social initiatives and businesses are usually ahead of official undertakings. Groups of urban and social activists have long been involved in activities aimed at protecting the cultural and material heritage of Königsberg and Eastern Prussia. Among them is a group of activists known for its motto "Let's save the pavement". It protests against the destruction of Kaliningrad's pre-war pavements.

Another initiative, "The Avenues of the Kaliningrad Oblast", gathers together people who, as the name suggests, want to preserve pre-war avenues. The local authorities have, in recent years, been trying to cut down the trees that grow along the pre-war streets. The arguments used by the government were pointing to security reasons. In addition, numerous initiatives have been undertaken in Kaliningrad which have been modelled on western examples. They include projects such as walking tours, during which guides and local specialists journey together with residents while re-discovering the traces of the city's pre-war history, as well as lectures, competitions and public debates. Such debates often take place at the Sackheim Gate (Sackheimer Tor), which is one of the preserved city gates which has been turned by a group of enthusiasts into a cultural and artistic space. Other interesting initiatives include a private museum, Altes Haus, which is to be found in a flat of a 1907 building and which displays numerous pre-war objects and organises meetings on Königsberg's culture.

References to history and the pre-war aesthetics are also exploited by local businesses. A good example is the network of bakeries and cafés called Königs-bäcker. Interestingly, to Russians who do not speak German or understand the context, this name is completely incomprehensible. The entity that is responsible for creating the visual identity strategy, which refers to the region, is Pictorica, a company which publishes books and albums on the city's history and designs unique souvenirs. Overall, many different businesses make visual references to Königsberg. Restaurant and shop interiors are often decorated with wallpapers showing pictures of old Königsberg. These displays can also be seen at bus stops and kiosks. Restaurant menus and decorations which reference Königbserg are an old phenomenon in Kaliningrad. However, the most striking are the loose architectural references, which at times take strange forms, such as an entertainment complex called "The Royal Residence" or the "Nesselbeck" castle. The aesthetic value of these objects is questionable, but they perfectly illustrate how important the city's German history is, as well as the role it plays in making the region seem more attractive, even when it is used in an unrepresentative manner.

Conservative groups warn against the Germanification of Kaliningrad, framing it as an element of the hybrid war being waged by the West against Russia.

Clearly, not every group that is interested in the pre-war history of the city is happy about these developments. To describe the current process of cultural rediscovery taking place in Kaliningrad, Andrey Vypolzov, a journalist with the Russian press agency Regnum, came up with the term "creeping Königsbergisation", a phrase that is becoming increasingly popular. Conservative groups are using it in a hostile way, warning against the Germanification of the Kaliningrad Oblast and framing it as an element of the hybrid war being led by the West against Russia. Liberal circles are equally happy to use it, albeit in an ironic context.

Our beloved city

The reconstruction of the Royal Castle is being accompanied by an increase in Russian and Soviet elements, which are resonant of the "Russian Spring", meaning a patriotic consolidation inspired by certain political changes taking place in Eastern Europe, such as the EuroMaidan Revolution, the annexation of Crimea and the war in Donbas. At Victory Square, where in the 1990s the Cathedral of Christ the Saviour was built, a ten-meter monument of St Vladimir is to be erected, while the anniversaries of Königbserg are not being celebrated.

Instead, every year the media covers the anniversary of the city's takeover by the Red Army in 1945 and the official Days of the City are celebrated annually in early July, to commemorate the transformation of the city from Königsberg to Kaliningrad in 1946. In 2016 Kaliningrad held festive celebrations marking the 70th anniversary of its existence. Year after year, just like in mainland Russia, Victory Day is celebrated in Kaliningrad on May 9th. In 2016 the March of the Immortal Regiment, according to data collected by the city council, involved 30,000 people, and taking into account the never-ending stream of people carrying images of their predecessors and relatives fighting in the Great Patriotic War, this number sounds very plausible.

Kaliningrad residents are also happy to repeat a popular rhyme *"Спасибо деду за победу"* (thank you Grandpa for the victory), to which they add "and our beloved city". This slogan shows that they understand perfectly well where they came from and who they owe it to. The "Great Victory" over fascism is a founding myth for Kaliningrad. By contrast, Königsberg is something that has been left over. It functions in parallel; or even more so, in the background of the city.   NEE

Translated by Iwona Reichardt

Paulina Siegień is an ethnographer, Russian philologist and translator. She is a graduate of the Centre for East European Studies at the University of Warsaw and is currently pursuing her PhD at the University of Gdańsk.

Making sense of what was left behind

A walk with Professor Jonathan Webber through the exhibit *Traces of Memory. A Contemporary Look at the Jewish Past in Poland,* Galicia Jewish Museum in Kraków. Interviewer: Iwona Reichardt

IWONA REICHARDT: Can you tell me about the origins of this exhibition?

JONATHAN WEBBER: I first started coming to Poland as a guest of the Institute of Sociology of the Jagiellonian University in Kraków in the 1980s. As a scholar-in-residence at the institute's summer school I started visiting many villages and small towns that were once vibrant Jewish communities. I was astonished as to how much of what I found was in poor condition. I collected a lot of material in different localities, restricting myself, however, to the borders of the former 19th century province of the Austro-Hungarian Galicia. I only worked within its Polish part, between Andrychów and Przemyśl. I came here every summer.

In 1993 I was approached by a British photographer named Chris Schwarz. Chris took photographs of the many places that I had researched. In 2004, as a result of our collaboration, the Galicia Jewish Museum was opened in Kraków

with its permanent exhibition entitled "Traces of Memory". Chris passed away in 2007.

This year, almost a decade after his passing and more than fifteen years after the first photographs were taken, we have updated and extended the core exhibition, which is now open to the public as "Traces of Memory. A Contemporary Look at the Jewish Past in Poland". This exhibition includes Chris's original photographs along with photographs of another talented photographer named Jason Francisco.

Why did you decide to update the original exhibition that you put together with Chris Schwarz?

Since the opening of the museum and the first exhibit that we prepared with Chris, more research was taking place in regards to the Jewish past in Poland and more books were being written on the subject. Today we know a lot more about the towns and villages where Jew-

Photo by Ada Kopeć-Pawlikowska

Professor Jonathan Webber, co-author of the exhibit.

ish life once existed in this region than we did 15 years ago. Initially, these localities did not encourage interest in their Jewish past. But that has changed, and that is why we had to update and expand the original exhibition to include new photographs.

During the press conference which launched this exhibition you said that it is an exhibition of ideas. What do you mean?

When I worked with Chris on the original exhibition he asked me in which order we should arrange the photographs. As this exhibition is not a historical exhibition it did not need to be arranged chronologically. Thus we decided to arrange the photographs thematically. We have done so because when many people think about the Jewish past in Poland, they think in very stereotypical ways. They think of Polish antisemitism, or Polish complicity during the Holocaust. The purpose of this exhibition is to force you not to think in such a stereotypical way. You are forced to understand the complexity of the subject. To make this complex theme accessible to ordinary people who come to visit this museum, I came up with five themes on which to arrange the photographs and which I completed with captions.

Photo by Jason Francisco / Courtesy of Galicia Jewish Museum

A grave of a Jewish family and Jan Janton, a Polish Catholic, who provided them with food and shelter. Janton was betrayed by a informer and killed together with the Jews in 1942.

Before we walk through these five sections, let me first describe the photograph that opens the exhibition and that presents a lone tombstone in Płaszów (Kraków). When you look at it, it is obvious that you are looking at a tombstone. Obviously, there must have been a cemetery in this place, yet there is no evidence of one. Thus, we can say that this prewar tombstone is a lone surviving trace of memory. It shows the randomness and complexity of the surviving traces of Jewish life in Poland. It is a symbol of both the catastrophe and the challenge we have today in trying to make sense of what was left behind.

Let me make one more important point: Poland today has one of the smallest Jewish communities in the world which, before the war, was one of the largest in the world. This shows the difficult history that is being memorialised today. To capture the complexity of Jewish history and memory we start the exhibition by setting up some key points, in which we state: 1) Jewish history in Poland is very long, 2) just a few remnants have survived and 3) there are museums that really try to present this past in a very respectful and dignified way. We are in one of them. As I have said before, this is an exhibit about ideas...

What is idea number one?

Idea number one is that the post-Holocaust Jewish world in Poland is in ruins. It is a very shocking way to begin an exhibition. We show that it is entirely in ruins. This is seen immediately in the photograph of a synagogue in Wieliczka or the metaphorical photograph of an empty main square in the small town of Biecz. The building with the arched doors and windows that is captured on the photograph was once a synagogue. Now it is a library. When you look at this photograph you know that there are people who live in Biecz, but you do not see them in the photo. The square is empty. In a very metaphorical way this photograph illustrates the idea of Jewish absence.

Other photographs in this section, like the ones from Rymanów, Dąbrowa Tarnowska and other locations (even one in Kraków), show synagogues which are (or until very recently were) in ruins. We see their sad fate; their past greatness and present desolation. As a matter of fact when we look at the photograph that presents a synagogue without a roof we can say that we are looking at a photograph of the Holocaust. This now ruined synagogue was once a beautiful piece of architecture, a true gem of its time. Its devastation is a testimony to the destruction of a great civilisation. The Jewish people who come today to Poland and have a picture of the Auschwitz's "Arbeit Macht Frei" sign in mind, they have the wrong approach. Auschwitz was a German concentration camp and

"Arbeit Macht Frei" is a sign in German. Yet to show a ruined synagogue… that is a much stronger expression of the Jewish life in ruins after the Holocaust.

Let us now move to section two, which is in direct opposition and powerful contrast to the first section. In this section we show that while indeed there are ruins, there are also many Jewish monuments that have survived. Some of them offer excellent insight into the Jewish world in Poland and life that existed before the catastrophe. They show us the Jewish life and culture as it once was. Let us start with the beautifully painted synagogue in Łańcut. This is what the synagogue in Rymanów, the one that I had said was a symbol of the Holocaust, also looked like before. But now, we can see the difference between the two, while the latter is in ruins, the former is beautifully restored*.

And what is this building in Łańcut used for today?

It is a museum. So even if it is not being used as it was before, it is being used.

---

* The synagogue in Rymanów was restored after the photograph was taken. In the exhibit there are two pictures of the synagogue. Section two presents the original picture, taken by Chris Schwarz. It is meant to show the "starting point" and be a symbolic representation of the landscape of the Jewish life in Poland 25 years ago. The caption beneath the photograph informs that the synagogue has been restored. The second photograph of the synagogue was taken by Jason Francisco and is displayed in section four of the exhibit.

Photo by Jason Francisco / Courtesy of Galicia Jewish Museum

Interior of the synagogue in Dębica, now a market with cheap goods.

There is also a photograph of the Rema Synagogue here in Kraków, at Kazimierz. This is the oldest surviving synagogue in Poland still in regular use. Here we also show photographs from the town of Leżajsk, which was the hometown of the founder of Hasidism in Galicia and which until today is the destination of many Jewish pilgrimages. Another location of frequent Hasidic pilgrimages is the hilltop Jewish cemetery in Bobowa. Here is its photograph. Another telling picture is that of a cemetery in Lubaczów. You can see that the Jews had a beautiful tradition of tomb carving. Such art is no longer present. These old cemeteries tell

us also that Jews were not one culture. Some were more traditional, some were poor. Not all were so rich. Some tombstones were written entirely in Hebrew, others in Polish.

I have to emphasise that all the pictures that I have showed you in sections one and two have no people. The point is to show absence. Now, let us move on to another section, one which also does not have people and which presents the sites of massacre and destruction during the Holocaust. This section shows that the Shoah did not take place solely in large concentration camps. It also took place in little known communities or

Photo by Jason Francisco / Courtesy of Galicia Jewish Museum
A destroyed synagogue in Przemyśl.

in forests and such sites can be found throughout Galicia.

Like the forest in this photograph?

Yes, exactly. This is a shocking photograph of a mass grave of 800 children located in a forest in Zbylitowska Góra, a few kilometres outside Tarnów. It is a site of a massacre. The children who were brutally murdered here were all from an orphanage in Tarnów. We will never know their names but their grave is a defining mark of genocide. Poland has hundreds, if not thousands, of such locations. Some of them have been completely forgotten. As you see, this section

starts very strongly, on a small scale in unfamiliar locations. But we also want to show that it is not true that all the Jews were killed in Auschwitz. They were murdered in villages, forests and also other lesser-known camps. You cannot compare them with Auschwitz, but they existed nonetheless.

The same can be said about the site shown in this next photograph. It is a photograph of Bełżec, a place where a half million people from all over Galicia were murdered in 1942, nearly all Jews. I call it the principal graveyard of Galicia. The Germans destroyed all evidence of the crime. There were almost

Photo by Jason Francisco / Courtesy of Galicia Jewish Museum

Bimah (central part) of the Old Synagogue in Tarnów. The synagogue was burnt by the Nazis in 1939. In 1987 the Bimah was covered with a roof.

no survivors. Many people survived Auschwitz, but not Bełżec – at most ten. There is only one memoir written about it. And that was not translated from Polish into any other language until the year 2000.

Obviously, we have photographs of Auschwitz as well. We present the entrance to the camp with the sign "Arbeit Macht Frei", but we show the camp's vast size as well as the ruins of the gas chambers and crematoria. When we show the interior of a gas chamber, we do not provide our visitors with numbers. We show the tragedy of the innocent children who were killed there. In the caption I quote Rafael Scharf, an essayist and a literary scholar from Kraków, recounting a Jewish mother and child's conversation before their execution in the chamber. Thus, you can read: "Mummy, when they kill us, will it hurt? No, my dearest, it will not hurt. It will only take a minute. It may have only taken a minute – but it is enough to keep us awake till the end of time."

Take a look at this photograph of the River San, which was an escape route for many Jews who were trying to get out of German-occupied Poland. A substantial number of them reached Soviet territory and hence survived the Holocaust.

Photo by Jason Francisco /Courtesy of Galicia Jewish Museum

Jews and Catholics coming together to commemorate the Holocaust at Zbylitowska Góra.

However, we must also remember that some were taken to the Gulag or were killed during the escape. Thus, the river is also a massacre site.

Of course, we could not avoid the topic of Polish complicity. We have two photographs that tackle this issue. One is from Gniewczyna, where 16 Jews were pushed into a house. Women were raped, and they were robbed and tortured. Poles

summoned them into a corner and called for the German police to murder them. These atrocities were relatively rare, but they did happen. You may explain them with Polish antisemitism but this is not enough because in Gniewczyna some Poles sheltered and rescued Jews. And to be antisemitic is one thing, but to rape and torture is something else. So antisemitism does not entirely explain everything. It was a similar atrocity as what happened in Jedwabne, which is mentioned in the caption. There were Polish collaborators in the hunting down and murdering of Jews. We have documents on that now.

On the other hand, look at the picture of this grave. It shows something opposite. There were Poles who risked their lives to save Jews during the Holocaust. And this is an interesting case of a Catholic Pole who hid some Jews in an underground shelter in the forest. He was betrayed by an informer. The Germans who arrived shot the whole group and he was also killed. So, as we see in this section there were both Poles who risked their lives to save Jews and Poles who collaborated with the Germans.

As we have finished walking through these three sections, in which we looked into the Jewish past, we will now move on to section number four, which focuses on how this past is being remembered today.

Would you say that what you showed me in section three was a shared Polish-Jewish tragedy? Can we regard them as a shared experience?

This is very difficult to say. There were places during the Second World War where Poles were murdered and places where Jews were murdered. So we have separate sites for them, but, as in this photograph of a monument in Tarnów, which we present in section number four, they were also mixed together. So the question is rather to what extent it was

a shared experience? We can have two monuments, two narratives, or one place with two completely opposite messages.

While walking through the fourth section, I would like to point out a photograph of Maria Dzik's grave at a Catholic cemetery in the small town in Tuchów, south of Tarnów. We have no physical evidence that there was once a Jewish community here, with the exception of the inscription on this tombstone, which says "Basia – Israel". Basia has left a trace that there was a Jewish community in Tuchów.

The exhibition also shows that while there are places like Przeworsk, which has an operating bus station in the place that was once a Jewish cemetery (just look at this shocking photograph taken by Jason Francisco where you can see a meaningless piece of concrete), there are also Jewish cemeteries that have been well restored, like the one in Brzostek. So in these two pictures, Przeworsk and Brzostek, you see both an erasure and restoration of memory. And this is true for so many other places. Another example is the synagogue in Dębica, which has been turned into a market with cheap goods, or the synagogue in Kalwaria Zebrzydowska which is now a furniture shop. And here is a synagogue in Dukla, which may not have a roof, but it has been nicely preserved as a public monument. There are also synagogues that have been restored with EU funding like the one in Dąbrowa Tarnowska. The last picture in this section is also very telling, it shows empty chairs at Plac

Bohaterów Getta, here in Kraków. They symbolise the Jewish absence.

Can we really talk about the absence as we are here in Kraków's Jewish district – Kazimierz?

The previous sections indeed had places, but no people. But to respond to your question, let us move to the last section where we show people. With the photographs that are here we say that the Jewish absence has been replaced by a new Jewish presence. There has been a revival of Jewish life. To express it we have included pictures that have not only been taken by our photographers of Jewish sites, but also by other photographers. Hence, you have photographs of Jewish celebrations: a circumcision or a Jewish wedding. There is a photograph of Jews and Catholics coming together to commemorate the Holocaust. You have photographs of the March of the Living, Holocaust survivors and the Jewish Cultural Festival. In other words, the Jewish life as it is today.

To summarise all that we have seen together I want to express what I hope to achieve with this unusual exhibition of ideas. It is my goal that people who come to visit this museum come out of the exhibition understanding how complex this subject is. There are some beautiful things to it, but there are some disturbing ones as well. Despite the difficult past, Jews have again become visible in this part of the world. Yes, the Jewish life here is in ruins, but it is not extinct. NEE

Jonathan Webber is a British social anthropologist with special expertise on European Judaism and European Jews. He taught at the University of Oxford, the University of Birmingham and Jagiellonian University. Professor Webber is the chairman of the Galicia Jewish Museum and a member of the International Auschwitz Council. For his services to Polish-Jewish dialogue he has been awarded the Gold Cross of Poland's Order of Merit.

Iwona Reichardt is a deputy editor-in-chief of *New Eastern Europe*. In preparation for the interview and while working on its final version, she also used the book *Redisvoering Traces of Memory. The Jewish Heritage of Polish Galicia* by Jonathan Webber (2009).

Jason Francisco is a photographer, essayist, curator, and educator. More information about his photographs, texts and projects can be found on his website: www.jasonfrancisco.net.

Where does an article end and a story begin?

HEKTOR HAARKÖTTER

The trend for journalism to move from reporting facts to telling a story based on facts is becoming increasingly recognised by German media. This trend is best illustrated by the conflict in Ukraine, where German journalists were able to tell the story of the war through the prism of a heroic tale of good versus evil.

The relationship between German journalism and its readers has been significantly disrupted over the last several years. Misreporting and hoaxes have frequently been identified, even in highly-respected news programmes published by public broadcasting channels, which used to be regarded as the flagships of German "quality journalism." The situation became especially evident during coverage of the civil unrest and Russian intervention in Ukraine. TV reports confused Ukrainian and Russian soldiers, transmitted unverified material and misidentified dates and times. Populist right wing movements have made particular use of these circumstances to launch an attack against the free press. The most prominent of these groups has been Pegida, which claims to be the sole ambassador of a patriotic Europe. The name Pegida is an acronym for "Patriotische Europäer gegen die Islamisierung des Abendlands" (patriotic Europeans against the Islamisation of the Occident) and one of their tactics is to accuse journalists of representing the "liar's press" or "Lügenpresse."

This simplification fails to recognise the real challenges faced by journalism today. When news bias occurs, it is not just a matter of publishing lies. A better explanation for the malpractice, or even malfunction, of German journalism can be found in the winding paths of its narratology.

What is a story?

The first ascertainment is that in principle, journalism is telling stories. Storytelling in this sense does not necessarily mean fiction. Once we accept that there are both fictional and factual stories then most forms of journalism can be understood as a type of storytelling. Therefore, narratology as the theory of storytelling can help us understand not only how journalists tell stories, but also which stories they will tell and which ones they will not. Naturally, in factual storytelling, the facts must be true, lest the story become fiction. However, there are also other laws of storytelling which are sometimes more important than the commandment to tell the truth.

The most important question of narratology is: What is a story? In the words of the French narratologist and structuralist, Gerard Genette, a story is basically the expression of a conflict between at least two people over a given period of time. Even if this definition seems to be quite simplistic it already contains explosive material in the debate regarding journalistic storytelling: the two people can be identified as a protagonist and an antagonist. Therefore, when it comes to journalistic inquiry, a reporter will first of all look for those two main characters.

With the concept of conflict, we then touch on the most widespread theory in journalism. At the starting point of journalism studies in the 1920s Walter Lippmann wrote about the theory of news values for the first time in his famous book *Public Opinion*. Lippmann answered the difficult question of which news items should actually make the news. In other words, out of the thousands of events that happen around the world every day, which ones should end up in a report in the newspaper or on TV or radio. With a catalogue of attributes, which events are considered worthy enough to warrant a place in the news? This is where the term "newsworthiness" originates from.

Lippmann's theory was further elaborated upon by Norwegian scholars Einar Östgaard, Johan Galtung and Mari Holmboe Ruge who, interestingly enough, were not specialists in communication but researchers in peace theory. They investigated why such self-evidently important issues as the destruction of mankind by nuclear weapons only occasionally found their way into newspapers. In their empirical analysis of newspaper reports about war in the 1950s and 60s, they found that besides criteria such as big names, locality, unexpectedness or continuity, the concept of conflict and competition is a major one. Without a considerable conflict, there is no news to tell. This is also the reason for the negative slant that most journalism seems to have: since we perceive conflicts to be negative, we also evaluate stories about them as negative.

The new lack of clarity

Competition marks the intersection between journalism theory and narratology: news, like stories, needs conflict and opponents. The difference is that while classical journalism saw the value of news as the attribute of a given event, narratology made a conflict/narrative the core of the story. Journalistic inquiry in this sense is no longer a hunt for the largest amount of or best information but for elements to build a story.

> News, like stories, needs conflict and opponents.

The pros and cons of such an approach are clear. During times of information overload, gathering information is pointless. What journalists really need is a mechanism to filter and select information, which is what narratology offers. What journalists are looking for (and what they sell to their readers/customers) are not events or information, but stories. Filtering information through the lens of storytelling means always getting a good story, i.e. a good product. On the other hand, the suspicion that journalists tend to dress up their stories in order to create a good product rather than a true and fact orientated report is justified.

What does all this have to do with the German journalistic misbehaviour during the conflict in Ukraine? That will become clear shortly. According to narratologist Joseph Campbell there is only one unique story. Campbell calls it the monomyth and identifies it as the quest. The quest is the journey of the hero to achieve a goal comparable to the tales of medieval knights questing to find the Holy Grail. The monomyth is a kind of template or archetype for storytelling. Lippmann stated that journalists often use stereotypes in their reporting through the prism of narratology, in that way one can identify those stereotypes as different storytelling archetypes.

The civil unrest in Ukraine and Russia's subsequent intervention highlight the typical problems of journalism. Before the conflict, Ukraine was barely mentioned in German media. It was not, to use the vocabulary of newsworthiness, an "elite nation" from the point of view of German journalism. German mass media foreign correspondents were not located in Kyiv, but in Moscow. Therefore, the new political circumstances in Kyiv led German journalists to a situation that German philosopher Jürgen Habermas once called "die neue Unübersichtlichkeit", a phrase that can be roughly translated as "the new missing overview" or, more accurately, "the new lack of clarity". Operating under these circumstances, narratology is a big help, as in recourse to archetypes and stereotypes, journalists are still able to tell a story, even when not in full possession of all the necessary facts.

An old stereotype in German history is that Russian leaders are aggressors, Russian soldiers are rapists and the Russian people are plainspoken, uncultivated, savage Asians. There are even people in Germany (thankfully, increasingly few) who are convinced that the Second World War was a German act of defence, rather than an offensive onslaught, despite Germany having invaded Russia and not vice versa.

Thus, the roles become assigned. The role of the opponent is played by Russia. Furthermore, since journalism, like narratology, prefers to personalise its stories, the Russian president, Vladimir Putin, plays the bogeyman. Some of the headlines found in the German press include: "Putin's secret army", "Putin prepares for the Third World War", "Against Putin, only heavy-handedness helps" and finally "Putin is breeding killer-dolphins". In October 2015 the well-known German news magazine *Der Spiegel* published a front page picture with Putin sitting in a fighter jet accompanied by the headline "Putin attacks".

Heroic tale

The role of the opponent is to frame the hero as the protagonist of the mono-myth. In this regard, German journalists had an ace up their sleeves. Vitali and Vladimir Klitschko, brothers and boxing champions, are both very well-known and highly regarded in Germany. Since 1996, they have both been under contract with a German boxing management company and also have multi-million dollar contracts from the biggest German private TV station, RTL. The brothers speak German fluently and, in a strange way, are widely considered to "belong" to Germany. Since Vitali Klitschko played a decisive role during the EuroMaidan Revolution, ultimately becoming the mayor of Kyiv, he is in every sense "the good guy" in this story. His muscular physique combined with his image as a "gentleman athlete" makes him look like a revenant of Rocky Balboa.

The coverage of Ukraine in the German press being conveyed as a heroic tale is even more perceptible in the case of female helicopter pilot Nadiya Savchenko, who was arrested by Russians. The German press, regardless of each outlet's political orientation, referred to her as the "Ukrainian Joan of Arc." Savchenko is the perfect example of journalistic reporting transitioning to fairy tale-like storytelling.

As in all fairy tales, people's dialectics fall by the wayside in favour of the tried-and-tested schematic of good versus evil; heaven versus hell. Despite the fact that it was the Svoboda movement, which contained some nationalistic/neo-fascist elements, that formed part of Arseniy Yatsenyuk's government in 2014, German journalists relegated it to the small print. It would have ruined the storyline and thus was widely ignored by the German press.

Journalism as a form of storytelling describes the blueprint of journalism on the whole. In his study titled *Mainstream*, German communications scientist Uwe Krüger argued that many journalists follow a political mainstream, which, unbalanced, tends towards supporting the government opinion. In his detailed network analysis, Krüger pointed out that leading German journalists (also called "alpha-journalists") are engaged in "pressure groups" that are unilaterally connected to NATO and the United States, such as the "Atlantik Brücke" (Atlantic Bridge) or the "Bundesakademie für Sicherheitspolitik" (Federal Academy Concerning Security Policy), which belongs directly to the German secretary of defence. Krüger refers to another German communication scientist, Lutz Hachmeister, who stated nine years ago that politicians, economists and alpha-journalists have built a "closed shop". Hans Leyendecker, a legendary investigative reporter with *Süddeutsche Zeitung*, speaks of "conspiratorial entanglements". Finally Hans-Ulrich Jörges from the news magazine *Stern* calls the relationship between journalists and politicians in Germany "personal fraternisation with politics".

One must be silent

The decision making process regarding which stories are reported as news leads to many other important stories being ignored. In Germany sociologist Peter Ludes founded the Initiative Nachrichtenaufklärung (news enlightenment organisation), the German counterpart to the US "Project Censored". Every year, this organisation chooses a top ten list of stories that were ignored by the German mass media. After nearly 20 years of media criticism, empirical studies of these lists illustrate the factors that prevent stories from becoming news. Firstly, the more sophisticated the circumstances surrounding a story are, the less likely it is to be reported. Secondly, intellectual discourse and weighing up the pros and cons of data is simply not an interesting part of storytelling. That is the reason why the Syrian civil war all but disappeared from the German press as soon as Russia entered the conflict. As Russian troops battled against ISIS, the simple good versus evil narrative no longer worked.

Black and white storytelling no longer fits within the framework of a conflict that epitomises the word "confusing." Of course, journalism is supposed to make complex issues more readily digestible. However, in obscure situations such as the one in Syria, with its multitude of conflicting parties, religions and international interests, the prime directive of German philosopher Ludwig Wittgenstein holds true: "Whereof one cannot speak, thereof one must be silent."

It is the narrator who holds an important role in narratology, because it is he who gives focus to the story, evaluates the facts and judges the conflict. However, this model only fits when the narrator is not part of the story, or more importantly, not part of the conflict. For this reason, German journalists telling the story of the radical changes in Eastern Europe and Ukraine pretend not to be part of the game, even though Germany and the European Union are major players in Eastern Europe (and the Ukraine–European Union Association Agreement was the trigger that caused the revolution against Viktor Yanukovych). In the meantime, German readers get to hear about events taking place far away, without any form of personal involvement. The reason for this is not so much the facts that are being reported, but rather the journalistic language that is being used. Since it fulfils the requirement of objectivity all the reports about the conflict were told in a distanced manner.

> It is the narrator who holds an important role in narratology, because it is he who gives focus to the story, evaluates the facts and judges the conflict.

In his classical study *Metahistory: The historical imagination in nineteenth-century Europe*, historian Hayden White pointed out that historiography does not tell us "how it really was", but offers "a verbal structure in the form of a narrative prose discourse" connected to the rhetorical figures of metaphor, metonymy, synecdoche and irony. Even to this day, a theory of meta-journalism is still missing. This theory would, according to White's system, explain the working method of reporting as an act of narration. It is all about storytelling, not truth-telling. NEE)

Hektor Haarkötter is the dean of the faculty of journalism and communication at HMKW University of Applied Science in Köln.

EASTERN CAFÉ

An indictment rather than a biography

LUBOŠ VESELÝ

Stepan Bandera: The Life and Afterlife of a Ukrainian Nationalist. Fascism, Genocide, and Cult. By: Grzegorz Rossoliński-Liebe. Publisher: Ibidem-Verlag, Stuttgart 2014.

Grzegorz Rossoliński-Liebe's 2014 scholarly biography of more than 500 pages on Stepan Bandera is divided into ten chapters, each significantly different in length and manner of elaboration. Throughout the book, the author pays more attention to Ukrainian nationalism in general, or rather attempts to condemn it as a damnable phenomenon, than to Stepan Bandera or his movement. This makes the book both unclear and disinteresting.The entire text could be summed up by one thesis presented at length in the conclusion of the book: that Stepan Bandera was one of the "central figures of the revolutionary and genocidal

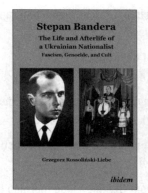

Ukrainian nationalist movement… after establishing the UPA (the Ukrainian Insurgent Army – editor's note) in late 1942 and early 1943, the [Organisation of Ukrainian Nationalist] became a partisan underground movement similar to the Forest Brothers in the Baltic states. However, yet again, it did not give up its fanatical and suicidal nationalism and did not cease killing civilians en masse … [Bandera's] most important achievement was to become the leader of a movement that tried to establish an authoritarian, fascist state and that attempted to 'cleanse' this state of ethnic enemies and political opponents, including Jews, Poles, Russians, 'Soviets' and even communist, leftist, conservative and democratic Ukrainians. Even if some of his ideals, such as protecting Ukrainians against Poles and Russians, might appear to have been noble, the methods he and his movement used should be exposed and criticised, together with their ongoing denial and euphemisation."

Fundamental problem

Herein lies the fundamental problem of the book: despite analysing nearly all the available literature, a number of Ukrainian, German and Polish archives and interviewing both Holocaust survivors and Ukrainian nationalists, the author resorts to outright condemnation, instead of aiming to grasp how it was and seeking an understanding and description of the motives and circumstances behind Bandera and the other Ukrainian nationalists' actions. Furthermore, Rossoliński-Liebe does not contribute to the understanding of why a substantial part of today's western Ukrainian population supported Bandera at the time and why he has become a symbol of the fight for independence for a considerable number of Ukrainians today. In the author's interpretation of events, Bandera's life disappears under a pile of descriptions and arguments that are supposed to prove that he and all Ukrainian nationalists were and still are antisemites, racists, fascists, collaborators, Russophobes and so on.

Despite Rossoliński-Liebe's forceful stance, his argumentation is shallow and considerably schematic. For example, he considers nationalism in general to be closely related to fascism. "Although nationalism and fascism were influenced by racism and antisemitism," he writes, "they were not racist or antisemitic to the same extent" and "although nationalism and fascism are distinct in nature, the boundaries between them became blurred, especially in the case of movements such as the OUN." The author does not assess Ukrainian nationalism

Rossoliński-Liebe does not contribute to the understanding of why a substantial part of today's western Ukrainian population supported Bandera and why he has become a symbol in the fight for independence.

in relation to Polish nationalism or in the wider context of its upsurge in Central and Eastern Europe at the end of the 19th and at the start of the 20th century, but sees it as something abnormal and pathological.

As Rossoliński-Liebe states in the introductory chapter of his book, "The political liberalism of the Habsburg Empire, as it developed after 1867, made Galician Ukrainians more nationalist, populist and mystical than eastern Ukrainians." In another section, he states that Galician nationalism was also more religious and spiritual, meaning that Ukrainians from lands other than eastern Galicia had serious problems accepting it. Even though he admits that some of Ukrainian nationalism's most important theorists, like Dmytro Dontsov or Mykola Stsiborskyi, were not born in Galicia (Dontsov came from Melitopol, situated on the left bank of the Dnieper, while Stsiborskyi, a leading OUN theorist, came from Zhytomyr), he repeats his thesis about "two Ukrainian identities" and about Ukrainian- and Russian-speaking parts of Ukraine many times throughout the book. He does so despite the fact that even after the Second World War, there were swathes of eastern Ukraine where Ukrainian was the only language that was spoken and that in many regions a mixture of both languages was (and still is) being used.

Ignoring context

In relation to Ukrainian nationalism, Rossoliński-Liebe uses expressive language and adjectives like "fanatic", "genocidal" and "suicidal". He writes phrases like national revolutions, national liberation, national liberation movement and independent Ukrainian state in quotation marks, explaining that in the OUN's and UPA's practice, these terms "could not have been liberation because it was not necessary to kill several thousand civilians to liberate Ukraine. The term 'liberation movement' suggests that the OUN and UPA were primarily devoted to the liberation of Ukraine. However, a study of the movement shows that the OUN and UPA were very much pre-occupied with the idea of 'cleansing' the Ukrainian territories of ethnic and political opponents." For the same reason, the author dedicated his book not only to his relatives, but also to the "memory of civilians killed by Ukrainian nationalism".

Ignoring historical context is a significant weakness of Rossoliński-Liebe's work. The vast majority of nation-states were born from the blood of innocent victims (to varying extents). The aim of all national or nationalist movements was to fight for a state, for a group of people who called themselves a nation and whose main characteristic, apart from sharing a misguided idea about their common past, was their hatred of their neighbours, as Karl Deutsch has shown. Before the Second World War, different nationalist, radical, right-wing, authoritative and fascist movements were on the rise throughout all of Europe. Therefore, the emergence of such a movement in Ukraine is not exceptional.

Similarly, the antisemitism in the movement was neither a Ukrainian invention nor something specific to Ukraine or its western regions. No matter how perverted this ideology is, it was spread throughout Europe, in particular in its eastern parts, where it took on an extraordinarily monstrous form. As Timothy Snyder brilliantly notes, after the outbreak of the Second World War and the collapse of existing institutions, in a region already plagued by various acts of violence and injustice, suitable conditions for even worse atrocities were created.

It is important to add that pogroms did not just happen in western Ukraine. Various people guided by different motives participated in them and they were not the domain of nationalists or, more specifically, Ukrainian nationalists or Banderites, as one might think after reading the book (even though they were also responsible for a number of heinous crimes). Moreover, one should consider the fact that Nazi Germany actively encouraged anti-Jewish acts and ethnic conflict. In addition, from a strictly formal point of view, the responsibility for murder lies with the occupying power,

> Before the Second World War, different nationalist, radical, right-wing, authoritative and fascist movements were on the rise throughout Europe. Therefore, their emergence in Ukraine is nothing exceptional.

in this case the Third Reich, as in Eastern Europe, there was no established independent or even quasi-independent state. For these and many other reasons, the allegations in the book that "the Germans, Ukrainian policemen, OUN and UPA and the local population killed almost all the Jews there [in western Ukraine]" are demonstrably incorrect.

Intentional oversights?

For Grzegorz Rossoliński-Liebe, Stepan Bandera and his followers are unambiguously fascists and Nazi collaborators. The author does not take into consideration either the arguments of renowned Ukrainian historians (for instance, he does not even mention Georgij Kasjanov's well-known article "The ideology of OUN: a historical retrospective analysis" from 2004), or the most widely accepted explanation of events in which both sides tried to exploit each other to achieve their goals. For reasons unknown, he also seems to consider Bandera to be the main supporter of collaboration with the Germans. He claims that the OUN leader Andrij Melnyk was no less eager than Bandera to collaborate with Nazi Germany. At the same time, he ignores the fact that the OUN's relationship to Nazi Germany was one of the primary causes of the split in Bandera's and Melnyk's wing of the Organization of Ukrainian Nationalists in 1940.

The author also overlooks Bandera's ambivalent relationship with the Greek-Catholic Church. Bandera was against closer co-operation with the Nazis and he insisted that the Ukrainian national movement should not be dependent on anyone. Therefore, it is a mystery why in the conclusion of his book the author claims that Ukrainian nationalists "were dependent on Nazi Germany, without whom they could not hope to establish and maintain a state. The OUN needed the protection of Nazi Germany and for that reason it collaborated with them and presented itself as a related movement." By propagating this argument, Rossoliński-Liebe achieves the same level of truth and insight on the matter as a comprehensive guide to the history of Ukrainian nationalism that was issued by the KGB University in 1955.

Although Rossoliński-Liebe focuses on current issues in Ukraine, he men-

tions the "growth of nationalism and right-wing radical activism that led to ethnic and political persecution and violence" and describes the building of the "anti-nationalist" monuments commemorating the victims of the OUN-UPA in eastern Ukraine, he does not write a word about the use of Bandera and Banderites in contemporary Russian propaganda, a development that has taken place since Vladimir Putin came to power. Such propaganda was used to discredit civil protests in Ukraine during the Orange Revolution in 2004 and even more so during the EuroMaidan in 2014. After the occupation of Crimea, Putin stated that the Ukrainian leadership is composed "of modern accomplices of Bandera" and on March 26th 2014, the Russian foreign ministry claimed in an official statement that "the Ukrainian radical right-wing forces extol Bandera and other Nazi henchmen". It is important to note that Bandera's reputation differs wildly, depending where in Ukraine you happen to to be. In the west, his legend is that of a fearless warrior. In the east, he is a fascist criminal and a mass murderer. Rossoliński-Liebe does not reflect either on why Bandera divided Ukraine so much or why he became such a favourite among Russian propagandists.

***

Rossoliński-Liebe unconsciously illustrates his clear misunderstanding of

Ukrainian and Eastern European realities in the conclusion of the book, where in an almost absurd paragraph, he asks a rhetorical question about whether "the political conflicts in 2013–2014 and the civil war in 2014 were in some way related to the Bandera cult and the apologetic attitude of some sections of Ukrainian society toward Ukrainian extreme nationalism." The author goes on to claim that "the rise of nationalism in western Ukraine and the inability to rethink Bandera and his epoch has contributed to the polarisation and radicalisation of post-communist Ukraine."

I will not even pass comment on the naming of Russian aggression as a "civil war", dividing Ukrainians into "western" and "eastern" and blaming "west-Ukrainian nationalists" for the polarisation and radicalisation of modern Ukrainian society. Even so, it is impossible to avoid the fact that in his evaluation of current events and in the vast majority of his theses concerning Bandera and Ukrainian nationalism, Grzegorz Rossoliński-Liebe's point of view sounds remarkably similair to official Russian propaganda.

Although the author's presentation of Bandera's life is ostensibly written in a scholarly manner, it sends a similar message to that of two previous Bandera biographies, one written by a former soldier named Oleg Smyslov which was published by a Moscow publisher and, paradoxically, a more interesting and more balanced popular-science biography written by Halyna Hordasevych and repeatedly published in Ukraine. However, for Rossoliński-Liebe, Hordasevych offers a "post-Soviet nation-

alist conclusion", as he calls it, without explaining what he means.

Unfortunately, the first academic biography of Stepan Bandera is a failure. The author has based his work on the conviction that his character and object of scientific research is a condemnable criminal. As for those who have recognised him as a national hero and a martyr (since 1959), both in Ukraine and in exile, for nearly all of the 20th century, they have merely covered up and legitimised his crimes. Ukrainian nationalism is evil and Ukrainians should give it up. Grzegorz Rossoliński-Liebe's book is a somewhat monotonous 600-page long indictment, not a biography.

Unfortunately, the first academic biography of Stepan Bandera is a failure.

For a considerable number of Ukrainians, Stepan Bandera is and always will be a symbol of resistance against Soviet Russia and Poland, as well as a symbol of the struggle for independence. Nevertheless, this does not mean that all Ukrainians agreed with his antisemitism, xenophobia, authoritarianism and use of violence as a means of political expression. For Rossoliński-Liebe, Bandera was and apparently remains a condemnable symbol of Ukrainian fascism, antisemitism, terrorism and an inspiration for anti-Jewish pogroms and even genocide. However, as a historian, he should not be committing such an abusive oversimplification, uprooting events and people from the context of the era or using harsh, unfounded and emotional judgments. 🖉

Translated by Olga Słowik

An extended version of this review was written for *Soudobé Dějiny*, published by the Institute for Contemporary History of the Academy of Sciences of the Czech Republic (Ústav pro soudobé dějiny Akademie věd České republiky)

Luboš Veselý graduated from the institute of international studies, faculty of social sciences at Charles University. He focuses on the modern history of Central and Eastern Europe. He currently works at the ministry of foreign affairs of the Czech Republic.

A test of otherness

ROMAN KABACHIY

Vielleicht Esther. Geschichten (Maybe Esther. Stories).
By: Katja Petrowskaja. Publisher: Suhrkamp Verlag,
Berlin, 2014 (Ukrainian edition, 2015).

"Not a single word in this book is redundant", said Natalia Gemenyuk, director of the Ukrainian TV-channel *hromadske.tv*, referring to *Maybe Esther*. Reading Katja Petrowskaja's family saga, you get the same impression. Maybe the reason is that you are afraid to lose the thread of the author's family story.

Personally, I had to muster up the courage to review this book, although it was Petrowskaja who had to muster up the courage first to write it and, before that, to decide that the truth and memory of her family were important to her. In one interview, she admitted that this story was written for her friends, ten people at most.

Therefore, I will start by explaining why, in my view, writing this book was difficult for her. Petrowskaja was born in 1970 and brought up in a totally Soviet spirit in the big city of Kyiv. Russian was her first language ("We were a Soviet family, Russian-speaking and nonreligious. Russian was a proud legacy for everyone who knew what desperation meant," she wrote) and she was ethnically Jewish (only one of her grandfathers was Ukrainian). The story of this family is the story of memories being wiped away, sometimes by family members themselves.

Discovering one's story

The title of the book *Maybe Esther* was an expression she had heard her father Myron, a writer who was quite well-known among Kyiv intellectuals, use about his own grandmother. He was not sure if that was really her name ("I called her grandma, and parents said mother"). This led to some research into the branches of her family tree, which takes us to Odesa, Kharkiv, Moscow and, of course, Kyiv. However, it also takes readers to Poland, specifically to Warsaw and Kalisz. In search of her inner self, Petrowskaja first looked to her childhood and youth. She recalls her grandmother Rosa's reaction to a Yiddish record she brought home from Poland in 1989: "My grandmother, who had not spoken a word of Yiddish in her life, suddenly broke into joyful song. I was listening to her and could not believe my ears. ... If not for this record, the sealed window of her early childhood would never have opened again to us and I would never have realised that my grandmother comes from a Warsaw which does not exist today."

Regarding why it was difficult for me, a Ukrainian and representative of a titular nation which had not been dominant in Ukraine for centuries, it was uncomfortable to realise that Jews had not only lost themselves (by accepting "higher" Russian culture, which was dominant in the cities), but also "assisted" in drowning us in that Russian sea. "I grew up in the family of fraternal people of the Soviet Union, where all were equal and everyone had to learn my mother tongue." Thus, there were equal and "more equal".

Apparently, I would still be "offended" had I only been brought up in the Ukrainian narrative. On the one hand, the Jewish population had to adapt and be subservient to the regional higher power (Jews faced a similar situation in the Polish Borderlands or Kresy, where they chose Polish culture, rather than Ukrainian or Belarusian). On the other, we Ukrainians, like the Poles, did not defend the Jews during the Second World War and neglected their presence. Those parallels manifest themselves in Petrowskaja's book, although they might seem artificial to some. The residents of Kyiv looked silently at the crowd of Jews who were to be executed at Babyn Yar shortly afterwards. Similarly, for a long time, Varsovians pretended that 39 per cent of the inhabitants of pre-war Warsaw need not be commemorated. Yet another example of the Ukrainian attitude to this matter is the fact that there is no department of Jewish studies at the local history museum in the city of Uman, one of the historic centres of Hasidism. This is apparently because "this museum is devoted to our country!" There is only room for the Ukrainian side of the story.

"People were killed here too"

Petrowskaja's book received high praise immediately following its release; first in Germany (20,000 copies sold in the first month) and then in the United Kingdom after it was translated. It has now been published in Ukraine, having been translated by Yurko Prokhasko, the brother of Ukrainian writer Taras Prokhasko and probably the best German-Ukrainian translator today. The book addresses topics including a fear of living in the Soviet Union and the lies of its official ideology; the underestimated role of a little man in the system; a disregard for the variety of people and their existence in the region; the fact that despite its proximity, Poland, a part of the communist bloc, was still very inaccessible; war and the manipulations related to them; and being a Jew in Eastern Europe, particularly during two periods of totalitarianism.

Both Katja and I, despite our eight year age gap, grew up during the era of stagnation in the Soviet Union. It was a time when there was no famine, war or mass repression (although dissidents were, of course, repressed). Thus, conversations about the misery of the previous decades sounded like fiction, something unbelievable to one of the last generations of Soviet children. Katja learned about Holodomor, the great famine, from her old neighbour, a Ukrainian woman named Makarivna. Since Makarivna was constantly drunk, her personal tragedies became intermingled. As a result, "the

war was to blame for everything and this was the only thing that was consistent with her reality".

Children went to the Victory Day parades to commemorate the victims of the war. However, exactly "who" these victims were, was a topic that slipped their minds. At the same time, the Soviet Union was fighting a real war in Afghanistan,

> Petrowskaja addresses such topics as the fear of living in the Soviet Union and the lies of its official ideology and the underestimated role of a little man in the system.

which was "far away" as far as the children were concerned. However, it became real for Katja, as she mentions in her book: "at the age of 10, I saw a zinc coffin containing the remains of our 19-year-old neighbour in front of our apartment block." This may have been one of the first insights the author had which led her to write the book over 20 years later.

Another blatant Soviet lie was concealing the truth about Babyn Yar. While the whole world was convicting Nazism of the Holocaust, we were neutrally speaking about "220,000 Soviet citizens" who died in a ravine. If you visit the location, you will not see that ravine. There is a park there, as if the place no longer exists. Thankfully, Petrowskaja describes the destruction of victims at Babyn Yar, portraying it as a place of killing and "burying, blasting, exhuming, burning, grinding, scattering, keeping silent, planting, lying, throwing garbage, flooding, covering with concrete, keeping silent again, fencing, and arresting the mourners".

During the Soviet period, it was impossible to draw attention to the special character of the victims at Babyn Yar. After Ukraine gained independence, it seemed like this would finally happen.

However, each group of victims has its own memorial (in addition to Jews, there are Gypsies and Ukrainian nationalists, among others). Despite this, there is no common memorial: "This selection lasts even in the memory"! The Soviet commemoration of what happened was insufficient and individual ones do not ease the pain. However, keeping in mind the claims that have been raised in Poland, that not every Pole who was killed in the 1940s in Volhynia has his own cross, it is no wonder that Katja and her parents found epigraphs and crosses on the edges of Babyn Yar: "People were killed here too".

Assembling the puzzle

The Odesa branch of her family, the Sterns, went down in history thanks to the brother of Katja's grandfather Semen, whose alias was Petrowski, which he adopted as his last name. Semen's brother, Judas Stern, shot at Fritz von Twardowski, the German ambassador to the Soviet Union, on March 5th 1932 in Moscow. The occasion could have been a trigger for war. Judas was executed after his rather ironic conduct in the court. This case is so striking to Katja that she wrote: "Judas had to be made up" as he fits the provocation so perfectly. Nevertheless, she is almost proud of his bold conduct. Although this genealogical branch is a dead-end, it contradicts the stereotype that "Jews only built Bolshevism". Of course, there is something to

this view as well. Myron's brother Vil (Katja's uncle) was given his name as it was an abbreviation of "Vladimir Ilyich Lenin", and according to his passport, he was of "Russian" ethnicity (while Myron was recorded as a "Jew").

Finally, a few words about how Poland is portrayed in the book. Petrowskaja is fair in her assessment that the Polish language was like a gate into the world of Kyiv intellectuals, and Mykola Riabchuk (a Ukrainian intellectual who is also a member of this magazine's editorial board – editor's note) often repeats this on his visits to Poland. Although Petrowskaja's parents and grandparents could understand and speak Polish, she herself does not know the language. In fact, it goes beyond Polish: "I lacked the knowledge of any language of my ancestors: Polish, Yiddish, Hebrew, sign language; I did not know a thing about a shtetl, or even a single prayer." Her family wandered into Poland from Austria. Seven generations of her ancestors had been teachers for deaf people, and along with finding out her family story, Katja felt a need to learn some languages. She learned German while her brother learnt modern Hebrew, and she gained some understanding of Polish as well.

"When I was growing up in Kyiv, Poland, our closest neighbour, was an inaccessible but fairly foreign country," she wrote in *Maybe Esther*. I had very similar feelings back in my youth. It was only during my doctoral studies that I realised how closely linked Ukrainian and Polish history is. For Katja, this also meant a search for her own past: "I went to a Warsaw that had existed two epochs before me. In order to see something of that era, I had to ignore the ruins that ran between now and a hundred years ago." She was annoyed that any mention of Jews in the Polish capital would inevitably lead to the ghetto and the Ghetto Uprising ("You pronounce two words, "Warsaw" and "Jews", and everybody immediately talks about the ghetto, as if there were an equation whereby Warsaw plus Jews equals ghetto").

She wanted to find some signs of the turbulent life of the Warsaw Jewish community which had created its culture and films in Yiddish. "At times, I felt like I was making my way through the debris of history," she wrote. Nevertheless, Katja found what she was seeking on Ciepła Street; where her great grandfather's school had been located, both physically and in photos. She wrote: "As a tourist, you have to choose which catastrophe you come to this city for: either the Warsaw Uprising or the Ghetto, as if there were two separate cities. Indeed, some believe that there were." In any event, Poland revealed its secrets to the author. (NEE)

Translated by Olena Shynkarenko

Roman Kabachiy is a Ukrainian historian and journalist.

In the mythical land of Armenia, the suffering is far from over

AGNIESZKA PIKULICKA-WILCZEWSKA

Armenia. Karawany śmierci (Armenia. The caravans of death).
By: Andrzej Brzeziecki and Malgorzata Nocuń. Publisher:
Wydawnictwo Czarne, Wołowiec, Poland, 2016.

When the "four-day-war" between the Armenian-supported forces and Azerbaijan erupted in Nagorno-Karabakh on April 2nd 2016, the world received a painful reminder that the old wounds in the southern Caucasus have not yet healed. With the death toll estimated at 350 people, the confrontation has shown that the unfinished business between the two countries has the potential to cause more suffering and further destabilise the region. The volatile ceasefire restored the status quo, although now that Russia's role in the mediation process has been enhanced at the expense of the OSCE's Minsk

group, the future remains far from certain. The mutual unrest, memories of ethnic cleansing and territorial disputes between Armenia and Azerbaijan form a part of a difficult shared memory. The renewal of hostilities has created yet another scar in their thorny relationship.

Even so, the Nagorno-Karabakh conflict, which has lasted for most of the previous century, is only one of a number of traumatic events in the memory of the Armenian nation. Locked between long-time foes Turkey and Azerbaijan and bordering Georgia to the north, Iran to the south and with Russia in close proximity, the country's position has been greatly influenced by great powers and geopolitics in the region. The recent book by Polish journalists Andrzej Brzeziecki and Malgorzata Nocuń titled *Armenia. The caravans of death* seeks to examine the nature of modern Armenian identity and address the various traumas of the nation's past. A series of feature stories, written by knowledgeable authors who have experienced Armenia, show how painful memories and a difficult present intersect to form a strong identity and shape the nation's collective memory.

Armenia. The caravans of death seeks to examine the nature of modern Armenian identity and address the various traumas of the nation's past.

The sky is higher

After the flood in the book of Genesis, Noah's Ark was said to rest on the top of Mount Ararat, a sacred place in Armenia. That is why Armenians came to believe that their land is the birthplace of modern civilisation. Although the mount is currently located on Turkish territory and the great days of ancient Armenia, the first country in the world to adopt Christianity, are long gone, the belief that Armenians are the chosen people in the chosen land is still rife.

"In Armenia, even the sky is higher", write Brzeziecki and Nocuń. The memories of ancient greatness have been accompanied by a history of occupation and plunder, which Armenia has experienced over the centuries at the hands of Arabs, Turks, Azeri, Persians and Russians. Without a continuous history of statehood, Armenians have found themselves living under various regimes, but have always managed to maintain a strong ethnic and Christian identity. In 1915 this distinctiveness served as a justification for the cleansing of ethnic Armenians, which led Raphael Lemkin to coin the term "genocide".

Fearing a pro-Russian diversion in the midst of the First World War, on April 24th 1915, the Young Turks government ordered the arrest of Armenia's intelligentsia and religious leaders. Although this was not the first example of ethnic strife and anti-Armenian propaganda, it was the first planned, institutionalised and large-scale effort to exterminate that nation. Following the introduction of a "deportation law", Armenians were ordered to make their way from Anatolia to Syria (which at that time was under Ottoman rule), where they were supposed to be placed in concentration camps. The arduous march, which came to be called "the caravans of death", saw hundreds of thousands of people die from hunger and exhaustion, while many women were kidnapped and raped. Turks and Kurds were called to massacre their Armenian neighbours and secure their belongings. "People were killed with knives, axes, swords and sabres; the killers were ordinary people, who would not have hurt a fly before the war. Even children were killing. People were possessed by the will to kill," one man recalled to Nocuń and Brzeziecki.

The genocide, which ended in 1917, constituted a defining moment in the history of the Armenian nation. In this respect, it is often compared to how the Holocaust has defined the Jews. As explained by Vamik Volkan, Emeritus Professor of Psychiatry at the University of Virginia, such traumatic experiences can be important factors in identity formation that can live on in the collective memory for generations, often in a mythologised form. While the genocide was supposed to exterminate the culture, spiritual and material values of Armenians, thus obliterating their identity, instead, it led to the emergence of a new one: that of Armenia as a victim.

Moreover, the fact that the extermination of Armenians has not been recognised as genocide by many countries, including the United States and Turkey, the perpetrator of this atrocity, has further strengthened the feelings of unrest, humiliation and historical injustice. As the authors of *Caravans of Death* were told by a woman who was too young to witness the slaughter, "The genocide intrudes on my life. It is a constant torment. I did not look at the slaughter, but the fear is in my blood. This is why I do not want to talk about 1915."

The enemy does not sleep

After the war in 1918 Armenia declared independence and in 1922 the Armenian Soviet Socialist Republic became part of the Soviet Union. This was followed by a period of relative calm, but violence erupted again once the first signs that the Soviet Union might fail began to show. The calls for the unification of Nagorno-Karabakh (a territory belonging to Soviet Azerbaijan) with Armenia, which started with protests in Yerevan in 1988, sparked ethnic unrest. Ethnic cleansing of Armenians in Azerbaijan (and vice versa) followed and both groups were forced to leave the other's territory. Seemingly overnight, people who until then had lived together in relative peace and friendship became worst enemies.

Then, in 1991, when the Soviet republics began declaring their independence from Moscow one by one, Nagorno-Karabakh followed suit. This activated a spiral of events which consequently led to a prolonged conflict between the two neighbours. Further escalated by hateful ideologies in both countries, the war left another traumatic mark on the history and identity of Armenians.

Although the ceasefire in 1994 halted military operations, the conflict is far from over, as the conflagration in April 2016 has demonstrated.

At the same time, as Nocuń and Brzeziecki remind us, the unresolved status of Nagorno-Karabakh is still on the political agenda, with the Armenian authorities frequently calling for national unity since "the Muslim enemy is not asleep". Despite this, in the Ararat brandy factory, there is a special barrel for reconciliation, which is meant to be opened only when relations between Azerbaijanis and Armenians are peaceful once more.

The 1915 genocide and the Nagorno-Karabakh conflict are the main historical traumas that helped shape the modern Armenian identity. However, the recent decades of freedom have also witnessed their fair share of tragic events. The grievous consequences of the 1988 earthquake, a long history of internal political violence, corruption, poverty and an increasing dependence on Russia have all left regular people angry, frustrated and disillusioned. Although, as the authors explain, Armenians are not cosmopolitan and leaving home is often seen as a tragedy, migration out of the country was and remains high. Those who left earlier as a result of genocide, war, starvation or poverty, pass their longing for Armenia, their mythologised vision of the country and their fears and traumas on to the next generations in the diaspora. For "Even those born in emigration miss their homeland", Nocuń and Brzeziecki explain. The country's current population is a state secret, but the economic situation has clearly pushed thousands to leave.

At the time of writing, radical oppositionists from the *Sasna Dzres* group are holding four policemen hostage after taking over a police station in Yerevan

> The 1915 genocide and the Nagorno-Karabakh conflict are the main historical traumas that helped shape the modern Armenian identity.

in a violent attack. They demand the release of their leader, Jirair Sefilian, who was arrested the previous month for plotting social unrest and attempting to overturn the government. It remains to be seen how the situation will end, but one thing is certain: in the mythical land of Armenia, where even the sky is higher, the suffering is far from over.

As Nocuń and Brzeziecki explain: "Pride and shame – these two feelings fight for a better place in Armenians' souls. For every argument about the greatness of this nation, one can find a counterargument showing its meagreness". NEE

Agnieszka Pikulicka-Wilczewska is an editor with *New Eastern Europe*.

On disappearance and deconstruction

ZBIGNIEW ROKITA

Wilimowski. By: Miljenko Jergović. Publisher: Książkowe Klimaty, Wrocław, Poland, 2016.

Miljenko Jergović is a man from the borderlands. He comes from the former Yugoslavia, has lived in Bosnia for a number of years and moved to Croatia during the war at the beginning of the 1990s. He is a fifty-year-old writer, poet and journalist, whose novel *Wilimowski* has just been released. Interestingly, the first country where the book was published was Poland. Why? On May 29th 2011 Jergović sent an email to about 25 different people with the text of the book attached.

In the email, he wrote: "It is currently unclear if it will be possible to publish this book in its original language. At the moment, there are no conditions for it…" Among the 25 contacts was a Polish diplomat and the translator of Jergović's books into Polish, a woman named Magdalena Petryńska. Together with a Polish publishing house called "Książkowe Klimaty", Petryńska ensured that the conditions were right in Poland for the book's publication.

Tragic life

This is not the only thing that connects the book to Poland. Ernest Wilimowski, whose name appears in the title of Jergović's book, was an international footballer born in Katowice, a Silesian town which came under Polish rule after the Second World War. Wilimowski's life was a tragic one. Before the Second World War, he became one of the Polish national team's biggest stars. Then after 1939, having signed a declaration proclaiming himself to be ethnically German, he became a sniper for the Third Reich. His tragedy was based on the fact that he never truly felt either German or Polish, but the historical moment in which he found himself forced him to choose. After the Second World War, he could no longer go back to Poland, while in post-war Germany, his extraordinary football talents were never discovered. He died forgotten in 1997 and the Polish Football Association ignored the funeral of possibly one of the best Polish footballers in history, sending neither a wreath nor its condolences.

Ernest Wilimowski was a Silesian. He was a representative of a nation which does not have its own state; a nation which has always consisted of borderland people, living across Czech, German and Polish territories. Its members speak various languages and have different historical memories. Jergović has a good understanding of the culture of borderlands. He saw evil in the Balkan Wars and knows the tragedy of nationalism, when all of a sudden, politicians do not allow for multiple identities. He writes about Wilimowski and the Silesians: "They are among Poles, Germans; among Germans, Poles … When a war erupts again and forces them to whittle down their identity to a single form and choose with good sense to belong to the group that will give them the greatest chances of survival, Upper Silesians will become murderers or martyrs…" Writing about Wilimowski's teammate: "In those years, Fritz Scherfke, like Ernest Wilimowski, said that when it comes to nationality, he is an Upper Silesian; neither a Pole nor a German. More accurately, he is both a Pole and a German." In an interview with the Polish daily *Gazeta Wyborcza*, Jergović sums it up: "Our problem in the 20th century was based on the fact that we could not live with others and we also could not live with ourselves. We were, and still are, the victims of a nationalist model of the world. In the understanding of a nationalist, a man can have only one identity, and if he has more, he is a traitor."

Jergović has a good understanding of the culture of borderlands. He saw evil in the Balkan Wars and knows the tragedy of nationalism.

Despite the title, Wilimowski is not the protagonist of Jergović's book, but merely provides the background to it. The action takes place in the summer of 1938, one year before the onset of the Second World War. At that time, the

World Cup football championship was taking place in France. The main protagonists of the book are a Jew, Professor Tomasz Mieroszewski, and his extraordinarily intelligent eight-year-old son, Dawid. Mieroszewski decides to move far away from his home in Kraków and listens to the championship broadcast outside Poland. His son is suffering from a terminal illness and does not have much time to live. We learn about the professor's decision: "It is easier to wait for death where grapevines grow and basil perfumes the air than in a country where only potatoes grow..." Thus, they choose to stay in a sleepy Balkan town at a small hotel run by an immigrant from Hitler's Germany.

Mieroszewski heard about the place from a poor, terminally ill Bosnian student whom he once met in Kraków, when the young man was reciting the poetry of Heinrich Heine ("He does not begin thick books because he does not know if he will reach the end ... And although he is a writer, he will not write a novel, just poems and short stories"). The Bosnian advises him: "When a war starts again, and it will start for sure, a terrible war, one has to hide in this boarding house."

In 1938 war was in the air. It was a time when a significant part of Europe ceased practicing democracy and the Central and Eastern European countries which had emerged after the First World War almost all gave in to the temptation of authoritarianism. Jergović knows that the moment the Yugoslav monarchy collapses, the fascist Ustaše and Tito's communists will take over.

Sensitivity and skill

Professor Mieroszewski arrives in the German house with his dying son and servants. He begins by constructing a radio so that he can listen to the broadcast of the World Football Championship. He could make a fortune from his invention, but he deliberately does not try: "His radio receiver, which was stronger, better and cheaper than the best German devices, could have revolutionised the electronics industry, but the coming months and years looked so gloomy and hopeless that he felt it would be a sin to create opportunities for people to carry their voices and music over such huge distances ... What could be carried with them at the time were the words of Mr Goebbels."

The climax of the book tells the story of a football match which took place in the afternoon on June 5th 1938 between Wilmowski's Poland and Brazil. Wilimowski scored four goals but Poland lost 5–6 and was eliminated. The match took place in the symbolic city of Strasbourg, which, unlike most cities, has a long history of changing hands.

Jergović's book is one of disappearances and repudiation. The old world is disappearing and the Second World War is destroying the contemporary order. The terminally ill Dawid Mieroszewski will disappear. The genial Wilimowski, who will become a German bureaucrat thanks to the war, will disappear. Silesians, who are looked down upon by Germans and treated equally despicably by Poles, will begin to disappear. Tomasz Mieroszewski, a Jew, will probably disappear too. Jergović's book is fantastic because thanks to the sensitivity and skill of his careful observation, the author succeeded in capturing the moment when the familiar world, both personal and collective, became deconstructed on a number of levels before our very eyes.

Today, Milijenko Jergović supports the English football club Liverpool. He formerly supported a team from Sarajevo, but stopped when Yugoslavia and the old Bosnia also disappeared. ⃝

Translated by Agnieszka Pikulicka-Wilczewska

Zbigniew Rokita is an editor with the Polish bimonthly magazine *Nowa Europa Wschodnia*.

Good night Ukraine, good morning Europe

FELIX ACKERMANN

Ukrainian Night. By: Kateryna Mishchenko
and Miron Zownir. Publisher:
Spector Books, Leipzig, 2015.

In 2014 I participated for the first time in a crowd-funding project for the production of a book on a post-Maidan Ukraine. After my initial payment, I forgot about the project and was consequently positively surprised to receive a hard-covered photo book titled *Ukrainian Night*, with a long essay attached. My first thought after reading the book was: "if the EuroMaidan in late 2013 and early 2014 was a revolution that gathered very different social strata, political positions, generational experiences and regional backgrounds,

an important question to ask is who was not symbolically represented at the starting point of a new Ukraine?"

The volume *Ukrainian Night*, published by Spector Books in 2015, uses this question as the starting point for an intensive journey with authors, Kateryna Mishchenko and Miron Zownir, throughout Ukraine. Both the text and the pictures focus on those who are invisible in the Ukrainian revolution of 2014. On a personal note, *Ukrainian Night* will not be my last crowdfunding experience.

Parallel worlds

The photo-essay ends with more angles of Maidan, with the barricades put up by people from almost all social and geographical spheres of contemporary Ukraine, demanding Viktor Yanukovych leave his post. Yet the book starts elsewhere. Mishchenko, the activist and writer, along with photographer Zownir, take the reader on a journey into the lesser known cellars, back yards and abandoned or destroyed public buildings in Ukraine. This is a country which is comprised not just of very different regions, but also of barely integrated social milieus which live in somewhat parallel worlds, unconnected by anything. With a weak state providing few resources to a broader share of the population, the edges of those social environments, who had participated in hardly any political discourse prior to 2014, did not become part of the new civil society that was proudly proclaimed during Maidan and materialised in the form of hundreds of voluntary organisations all over the country, facilitating support for internal refugees from Donbas and Crimea.

In *Ukrainian Night*, Zownir and Mishchenko present those who were not just excluded by the Ukrainian state, but who were also not included in the founding moment of a new post-Maidan Ukrainian nation. Both authors travel to Horlivka, Poltava, Kharkiv and Odesa. They cover the nightmares of the homeless and drug addicts, whose places of refuge are alcohol and narcotics. They take pictures of orphans who live in a parallel world and according to their own rules. In Ukrainian controlled territory Mishchenko and Zownir zoom into these semi-private spaces of despair. In Russian-annexed Crimea, they present the elderly, veterans of the Second World War and cover a parade of pride on May 9th.

Their photographic journey includes a picture of a beautiful, modernist Soviet chapel on the outskirts of Kyiv. It is not obvious why this picture was included. Was it for aesthetic reasons? Zownir also zooms in on the morgue in Poltava, showing the corpses of rather random people. This slightly fuzzy logic, which is also expressed by a rather chaotic

Ukrainian Night presents those who were both excluded by the Ukrainian state and omitted from the foundations of a new, post-Maidan Ukraine.

typography in a bold, barely readable font, takes the authors to the Zoo of Simferopol, which contains abandoned animals. They also travel further, to a Roma settlement in the border town of Uzhgorod. In a certain sense, the improvised typography and sometimes random set of pictures represent a time of upheaval, where Ukrainian society has

almost no time or will to spend much energy on contemplation.

A different Ukraine

The book is something of a field note diary, a documentation of a historical moment in which change is imagined as something civic, brought from below. By highlighting those who are at the bottom of Ukrainian society and who are not a part of any political processes, it also illustrates a serious obstacle to maintaining the post-Maidan euphoria. The message is clear: there is another Ukraine that exists separately from those who are socially mobile and willing to change their country.

The final part of the book on Maidan frames the text and gives it direction. The final statement and the Maidan pictures seem to suggest that it is up to Ukrainian society to re-organise itself, even in times of ongoing war fed by Russian troops and

military support. In doing so, Zownir's pictures sometimes zoom in closer than anticipated, pushing readers out of their comfort zone. Mishchenko's essay gives this journey into the Ukrainian night a sense of a search for the author's own point of view as an activist and writer, one who is deeply involved in the perpetuation of Maidan as an enduring historical event.

The strong black-and-white optics of the book show dark spots, where thousands of Ukrainian citizens remain in the shadow of recent Ukrainian history. The title *Ukrainian Night* anticipates its hypothesis: this is the night and there will be a new day, once the night is over. It challenges Europe to face the Ukrainian night, which is still not over. 🌙

Felix Ackermann is a research fellow at the German Historical Institute in Warsaw.

Kraków and Lviv
Two Cities of Literature

The relationship between Kraków and Lviv can be told in many different ways. Historians like to show their shared experiences and point to common heritage. Political scientists draw attention to the similarity of political culture that characterises the areas of the former province of Galicia. But it is the writers, poets, translators and culture managers whose works make Kraków and Lviv what they are today, namely the sole two cities from the region of Eastern and Central Europe that are now members of the UNESCO Network of Creative Cities.

Belonging to this prestigious club is not only the result of successfully passing an application process. It is an obligation to cherish, continue and carry into the future their centuries' long literary traditions. A task that both cities have committed to fulfil, as we read in the interviews with the founder of the Lviv Publishers' Forum, Oleksandra Koval, also known as the "good angel of Ukrainian literature", and director of the Kraków City of Literature programme Robert Piaskowski respectively.

It is also an opportunity to find common ground that trespasses some existing historical disputes and offer contribution to the pool of universal human culture. Thus, while Kinga Anna Gajda shows the presence of Lviv in Kraków's city walls, Natalka Sniadanko and Andriy Lyubka write about the existing and planned Polish-Ukrainian literary and translation projects, Adam Balcer unveils the lesser-known oriental face of Lviv that makes it more than a European city. We present these different dimensions of Kraków and Lviv today to tell the story about their relationship in yet another way.

Read on pages: 164–206

This section is co-financed by the City of Kraków.

Lviv Orientalis

ADAM BALCER

The city of Lviv is often perceived as a gateway to the West for Ukraine, alongside being proof of Ukraine's European heritage. However, the city's history as the intersection of key trade routes between Central Europe and Central Asia and the Middle East demonstrates its multi-cultural heritage which reaches far beyond that perception. Lviv is not only a European city; it is to a certain degree an Oriental one as well.

In the Polish and Ukrainian historical memory Lviv is primarily associated with maintaining close relations with the West. For Ukrainians, it is the part of the country that is the furthest to the West, not only in terms of geography but also with its culture. It is the best guarantee of Ukraine being a part of Europe. However, in Poland Lviv is perceived as a European bulwark, one that has, on several occasions, halted the marching of the Eastern Asian "hordes". This vision of the world is best illustrated by the inscriptions on the facade of Lviv town hall, which say: "Michael the Archangel saved the city of Lviv from the jaws of the Asian dragon." The inscription refers to the brief siege of the city by the Turks, Tatars and Ukrainian Cossacks which took place in 1672.

Nevertheless, Lviv was established and thrived thanks to its location at the intersection of key trade routes from Central Europe to Central Asia (West-East) and from the Baltic Sea, through the Black Sea, to the Middle East (North-South). As a result, elements of Muslim culture have become, both directly and indirectly, an integral part of the city's cultural landscape and have formed key characteristics of its original identity.

Proto-globalisation

The first mention of Lviv in historical sources appears in the mid-13th century. This was the time when the Mongol invasion resulted in the near total destruction of the Kievan Rus'. Even so, this area was included in the *Pax Mongolica*, spreading from the Carpathian Mountains to the Pacific Ocean and from the Baltic Sea to the Indian Ocean. Later, at the dawn of the modern era, the whole territory of Central and Eastern Europe was under the rule of two empires: the Ottoman Empire and the Polish-Lithuanian Commonwealth. The Ottoman expansion established *Pax Ottomana*, which turned the Black Sea into an Ottoman lake. In the north, the Ottoman Empire bordered the *Pax Respublica* created by the Polish-Lithuanian Union/Commonwealth. It was one of the largest European states ever to exist, stretching from the Baltic to the Black Sea. Throughout the Commonwealth's 400 year existence, it only fought against the Empire for approximately 25 years (mainly at the end of the 17th century). As a result, according to Fernard Braudel, a famous French historian, the Gdańsk-Lviv-Istanbul trade route was established.

These three historical processes led to the opening of unprecedented opportunities for trade development on a continental scale; a phenomenon that, can be called "proto-globalisation". The trade boom facilitated the migration of various ethnic groups and their integration with the native populations. As a result, since its earliest days, Lviv has been a multi-cultural city. People who settled there included Jews, Levantines (Italians from Genoa trading with the Middle East and the Eurasian Steppe), Armenians and Karaim and Tatar merchants. Along with the settlements came the temples of the Abrahamic religions that took root in the city: synagogues, a mosque and Armenian churches. Józef Bartłomiej Zimorowic, a mayor of Lviv in the 17th century, claimed that in the mid-14th century, the only place to resist the Poles was "Lviv, which was miraculously saved by … the Tatars, Saracens, Armenians and others who stood by the duke's side and hence it closed its gates to foreign dukes". Despite this opposition, when Casimir III the Great, a Polish king, captured the city, he paid tribute to the diversity of the city's inhabitants when he said: "Armenians, Jews, Saracens (Muslims) … and other peoples, regardless of their condition or class, while we grant them an extraordinary grace, we wish their rights regarding their religious rituals to be unaffected and remain as they are."

Even though they had been assimilated into the city's population by the first half of the 16th century, Muslims living in Lviv frequently visited Ottoman lands because of the city's strong trade relations with that part of the world. Martin Gruneweg, a 17th-century German merchant and chronicler from Gdańsk, compared Lviv to Venice: "In the city as in Venice, it became quite common to meet

> For Lviv, the Eurasian Steppe was its equivalent of the sea beyond the gate.

people at the market from all countries of the world in their dress: Magyars in magerkas, Cossacks in kuchmas, Muscovites with hats, Turks in white turbans. All of them are in long clothes. ... Each of them, whatever language they speak, find their own language here. The city is more than a hundred miles away from the sea. Yet when you see crowds of Cretans, Turks, or Italians dressed as sailors, you get the feeling that a seaport could be just beyond the city gate."

In Lviv's case, the Eurasian Steppe was its equivalent of the sea beyond the gate. However, the key difference between Lviv and Venice was that in Lviv, Muslims could move around freely and the influence of Islamic culture on art, clothing, cuisine, weaponry and language was much more significant. In fact, its influence was so strong that Lviv did not end up being merely a passive recipient of Muslim material culture; it also created it. Art historians called this cultural phenomenon the Lviv manufacture, which meant the onsite production of oriental products for domestic consumption. The most vivid example of this was a crafts factory in a royal townhouse run by Armenians, which was established by King John III Sobieski at the end of the 17th century.

Another great symbol of this cultural syncretism is the Renaissance altar in the Roman Catholic cathedral. The altar's ornamentation was inspired by the patterns of Persian carpets. Andrzej Dziubiński, a Polish historian, observed that the Orient also had an impact on Lviv's institutions: "some organisational Turkish (and more broadly Muslim) models were transferred onto the Polish, or more specifically, Lviv ones with regard to oriental trade. ... In the Ottoman Empire which, together with Islamic civilisation, took over numerous institutions from the era of the early caliphates, the organisation of the market and trading operations was supervised by a municipal official."

The East had to communicate with the West

Lviv's cultural melting pot became its trademark. During the interwar period, Stanisław Wasylewski, a Lviv-born, Polish journalist and literary critic, wrote the following about the city's historical heritage: "a multi-lingual Tower of Babel, although frequented by Persians, Greeks, Italians, Turks, Germans and Tatars who would come here to trade goods, was in need of translators. The East had to communicate with the West". Another chronicler, Józef Wittlin, wrote the following: "What is this bright-coloured crowd? It is Lviv. Diversified, multi-patterned, stunning like an eastern carpet. Greeks, Armenians, Italians, and Saracens all become Lviv-like among the Polish, Ruthenian and Jewish locals."

Relations between Lviv and the East did not end when the Russians conquered the Commonwealth and pushed the Ottoman Empire away from the Black Sea. During the interwar period, Lviv became a key Orient centre in Poland. For example, in 1922, the Polish Oriental Association was established in Lviv. Its journal, called the *Oriental Yearbook*, was launched in 1925 and was published in Lviv until the Second World War. One of the key professors who taught eastern languages at Lviv University was an Azeri named Sadykh Bey Aghabekov. He served as a general in the Russian Imperial Army and later worked as a deputy minister of internal affairs. He set up the police force in Azerbaijan, which was the first democratic and secular republic in the Islamic world. While serving in the Imperial Army, Aghebekov conducted studies on the culture of the Turkmen people of Central Asia. In Lviv, he published a Turkish and Arabic textbooks. He was invited to Lviv by Zygmunt Smogorzewski, a Russian, and later Polish, diplomat who worked as an oriental languages teacher in Lviv following his retirement from the diplomatic service and was the driving force behind Lviv's development as the centre of Polish studies of the Orient. Ali Ismail Woronowicz, a Polish Tatar who later became an imam in Warsaw and the chief Imam of the Polish Army, was also a student of these outstanding orientalists. In 1941 he was arrested and most probably killed by the Soviets.

No other nationality in Lviv contributed so much to its orientalisation as the Armenians

No other nationality in Lviv contributed so much to its orientalisation as the Armenians. Thanks to trade relations with their compatriots, the Armenians could do business from the Middle East to China. The greatest landmark and most important oriental symbol of Lviv which still stands today is the city's 14th-century cathedral, built by a Levantine Italian architect from Crimea. The building bears numerous characteristic features of Islamic art. Armenians came to Lviv from Crimea, where they adopted the Tatar language as their own, giving it a specific Armenian accent. They called the trade route from Lviv to Crimea "the Tatar route". Consequently, they were often associated with the Tatars, calling their language the Tatar language and often using Tatar-Muslim names. Although they maintained their Christian beliefs. Their weaponry, clothing and customs were also described as "Tatar". They identified with the Tatars to such an extent that the greatest Polish chronicler, Jan Długosz, claimed that the Tatars were the descendants of Armenians. Furthermore, in 1618 Armenians published the first book in the Turkic language in Lviv.

Intermediary between civilisations

Other Lviv residents had mixed feelings about such close identification with the Tatars. On the one hand, Lviv Armenians played crucial roles as Polish diplomats, translators and royal secretaries, as well as being general specialists on Turkey and Iran. On the other, according to the Polish historian Andrzej Zięba: "they were suspected of doing dishonest business with the Turks and Tatars and carrying out intelligence work for them. At the same time, their foreign descent, the Kipchak (Tatar) language and their trade relations in the Orient rationalised these prejudices."

The Armenian community in Lviv maintained very close relations with their compatriots from Turkey, Iran and even India. Minas Tohatetsi, born in Tokat in Anatolia, moved to Lviv and went down in history as one of the most significant Armenian poets and miniaturists of the 16th century. Another important figure was the 17th-century Armenian traveller Symeon Lehaci, who was born in Zamość but spent most of his life in Lviv. He is the author of a chronicle detailing numerous journeys in the Middle East that lasted several years. That chronicle has since become a unique source of knowledge about Armenian communities living in that part of the world. The role of the Armenian Lviv as an intermediary between civilisations is confirmed in the Bible of Lukas of Babert, which was written in Lviv. Its illustrations portray the Book of Revelations according to Albrecht Durer's woodcuts.

In the 16th and 17th centuries, Lviv Greeks were a major rival to the Armenians in terms of trade with the Ottoman Empire. Beyond that, the Greeks were a part of the Constantinople patriarchate religious community, which was subject to the Ottoman Emperor, not the Orthodox Church community in Ukraine. At the same time, Lviv was the closest large city in the Polish-Lithuanian Commonwealth to the Ottoman border. The most significant Greek merchant in Lviv's history was Konstanty Korniakt, who lived during the 16th century. He was originally from Crete but spent most of his life initially in Istanbul and then later Lviv. He became one of the wealthiest men in the Commonwealth. Even the king Sigismund II Augustus would borrow significant amounts of money from him. Korniakt helped finance buildings that later became symbols of Lviv: the chapel and the tower by the Dormition Church and the Korniakt Palace, the most beautiful example of Renaissance-style architecture on Ukrainian soil. Korniakt married into the Polish

and Ruthenian aristocracy. Moreover, he had a significant impact on the development of the Ruthenian community's religious life. He supported the establishment
of the Lviv Dormition Brotherhood, including its school and printing house.

The Greeks played a key role in the development of the Orthodox Church and
Ruthenian culture opposed to the Catholic counter-reformation and the notion of
a church union between the Orthodox and Catholic churches. The brotherhood
was also granted privileges under Jeremias II, the patriarch of Constantinople, who
had stayed in Lviv. The patriarchate's actions were supported by the Ottoman Emperor. Orthodox Christians considered him to be the
lesser of two evils (according to a well-known saying
at the time: "the sultan's turban is better than the Pope's
tiara"). On the other hand, as Igor Lylo, a Ukrainian
researcher, observed: "the Poles... had reasonable
grounds to suspect that the Greeks arriving in Poland
were secretly serving the sultan. Poles ... were extremely cautious, even towards the most important
representatives of the Orthodox Church" coming from
the Ottoman Empire.

> For the Orthodox Church, Ottoman rule was the lesser of two evils, as illustrated by the well-known saying: "better the sultan's turban than the Pope's tiara".

Today Lviv is a bastion of the church union and
Greek Catholicism. Paradoxically, of all the major
Ukrainian cities, Lviv stayed faithful to Orthodox
Christianity the longest, due primarily to its very strong ties with Constantinople.
The Polish authorities, concerned about the loyalty of the Orthodox Christians,
pushed for the union in Lviv.

Unique religious connections

For several generations, the Jewish community living in Lviv was made up of
three main groups: Ashkenazi Jews, Sephardic Jews and the Crimean Karaites. The
latter group spoke a language closely related to that of the Tatars; they came from
Crimea and are currently regarded as followers of a different religion to Judaism.
Sephardic Jews arrived in Lviv from the Balkans. However, they have roots in the
Iberian Peninsula where, for 800 years, they had been heavily influenced by Arabic
culture. Even though they came from the West, Ashkenazi Jews have their roots
in the Eurasian Steppe, as their name originates from the name of the Scythians,
Iranian nomads who had been living on the Eurasian Steppe since ancient times.
Since the Middle Ages, Europeans had perceived the Scythians to be the ances-
tors of all nomads, including the Tatars. Although Ashkenazi Jews originated from

Germany, they played an important role in the trade between Europe and Asia, along the route where Lviv was later established. They were called the Radanites, most probably a derivative of the Iranian word *rah-dan*, which means "one who knows the way".

Sephardic Jews in Lviv were concentrated around Yasef Nassi (also known as Joseph Nasi) and his commercial activities. He was an Ottoman diplomat (the sultan even bestowed him with the title of duke) with significant influence in the court in Istanbul and possessed great wealth. In exchange for a substantial loan, the Polish king Sigismund II Augustus granted Nassi numerous trade privileges in the Lithuanian-Polish Union/Commonwealth. He also played a significant role as a behind-the-scenes lobbyist in the election of Stefan Batory as Polish king.

The Crimean Karaites and Sephardic Jews gradually began to meld with the Ashkenazi Jews. Nevertheless, Sephardic culture maintained its influence over the Jewish community in Lviv as it was close to the border with the Ottoman Empire, where the majority of Jews were Sephardic. At the same time, the border between the Commonwealth and the Ottoman Empire was not an iron curtain and it did not separate Sephardic Jews from Ashkenazi ones. A good example is Zvi Hirsh Ashkenazy, one of the most prominent rabbis in Lviv's history. Zvi Hirsh was a descendant of Ashkenazi refugees from Vilnius, who fled the Russians in 1655 and found themselves in the Ottoman Empire. His grandfather was the Rabbi of Buda and Zvi Hirsh himself was educated in Ottoman Thessaloniki by Sephardic Jews, even though he originated from the Ashkenazi tradition. As a result, he was appointed Rabbi of Sephardic Sarajevo. His spiritual career was concluded in Lviv, where he died. Simon Ashkenazy was his descendant and became an outstanding Polish diplomat and historian during the interwar period. He is also known for establishing the Lviv School of History in Polish historiography.

> Relations between Muslims and Sephardic Jews in close proximity to Lviv resulted in the emergence of unique religious forms connecting Islam, Christianity and Judaism.

Relations between Muslims and Sephardic Jews in close proximity to Lviv, i.e. the border region of Podolia, which had even been an Ottoman province for a quarter of a century, resulted in the emergence of unique religious forms connecting Islam, Christianity and Judaism in the region. This phenomenon led to the beginning of Sabbateanism, a religious movement founded in the second half of the 17th century by Sabbatai Zevi, a mystic whose roots are in the Balkans. Zevi proclaimed himself to be a messiah. After being rejected by the Jewish community, he and his followers converted to Islam. Sabbatai's wife was a Jew from Podolia. The Sabbatean movement gave rise to Hassidism, a mystic stream in Judaism that adopted the rituals of Sephardic Jews and was founded in the 18th century in Podolia. Baal Shem Tov, its founder, was initially a Sabbatean follower.

In the second half of the 18th century, groups of Podolian and Lviv Jews migrated to the Ottoman Empire and, thanks to their relations with Sabbatean followers, converted to Islam. The most prominent among them was Jacob Frank, who was born in Buchach, outside Lviv, and raised under Ottoman rule. His mother tongue was Turkish. When he returned to Poland with his followers (the Frankists), he converted from Islam to Roman Catholicism and was ennobled. The conversion took place in Lviv and followed a famous theological dispute between the Frankists and the Judaists, during which Frank's speech had to be translated from Turkish.

The wide ranging influence of the Orient on Jewish Galicia was met with both reluctance and fascination by Lviv's inhabitants. The former is illustrated by the fact that Galicia was labelled "semi-Asia", mainly due to the strength of Hassidism, shaped by its relations with Islam. Lviv's fascination with the Ottoman Orient mixed with Hassidism found the most prominent expression in the works of Leopold von Sacher Masoch, a Lviv-born Austrian writer who presented himself as a descendant of the Spanish Moors. The term masochism, i.e. deriving sexual pleasure from pain and humiliation, is derived from his surname. According to American historian Larry Wolff, a fascination with masochism in Masoch's writings was related to his perception of the Orient through the prism of slavery, harem and despotism, things that the writer also saw in Galician villages.

Lviv was not only subject to the influences of the Orient; its people greatly contributed to major cultural transformations in the world of Islam and were important intermediaries between both civilisations. Lviv-born Ali Ufki Bej (alias Wojciech Bobowski, 1610–1675) was made a Tatar slave when he was a boy. He then became a dragoman at the court of the Ottoman Emperor (chief translator), as well as a musicologist and composer. It was thanks to him that Ottoman music was written for the first time using the form of European music notation. His collection of Ottoman musical pieces is invaluable to Turkey's cultural heritage. His works connected Ottoman and Orthodox Church music (before he converted to Islam, he was a Calvinist). Bobowski was the first person to translate the Christian catechism and the Bible into Turkish. He also wrote an explanation of Islam in Latin in order to acquaint Christians with Islamic rules, as well as translating the works of the most outstanding European Protestant thinkers, Hugo Grotius and Jan Amos Comenius, into Turkish.

While Bobowski might seem a distant historical figure, Muhamad Asad is much more recent. This brilliant Islamic theologian was born in Lviv in 1900 to a Jewish family. He was given the name Leopold to commemorate the city in which he was born (after he converted to Islam, he changed it to Asad, which is Arabic for lion). When he was 14, he moved to Vienna with his parents. In the 1920s, he converted to Islam and played a key role in the establishment of an independent Pakistan. Asad promoted the idea of reformation within Islam, as well as inter-religious dialogue. In 2008 the square in front of the UN Office in Vienna was named after him in commemoration of his work as a "religious bridge builder". In his autobiography, which was also his opus vitae, entitled *The Road to Mecca*, Asad included a poetical and metaphysical description of Lviv from his childhood, emphasising how much the city influenced his life. NEE)

Translated by Justyna Chada

Adam Balcer is the conference director at the College of Eastern Europe.

It is becoming increasingly common to find "book food" stands at hipster street food festivals in Lviv.

Photo by: Olha Mukha. Courtesy of Lviv UNESCO City of Literature

The real miracle of Lviv being granted the title of UNESCO City of Literature is that it was achieved thanks to the work of some very enthusiastic people.

Photo by: Kostya Beglov. Courtesy of Lviv UNESCO City of Literature

СИЛА
БЕЗСИЛИХ
ВАЦЛАВ ГАВЕЛ

ПАМ'ЯТІ
ЯНА ПАТОЧКИ

Even without any fancy titles, Lviv has always been a city of literature.

Lviv means literature

ANDRIY LYUBKA

"In the next life, I would like to be born as a Ukrainian poet" I heard a Swiss writer say. He looked quite captivated when a huge crowd of young people came to a meeting with him during last year's Publishers' Forum in Lviv.

Today, the UNESCO Creative Cities network connects 116 cities from 54 countries around the world. As the official webpage states, these are "cities that have identified creativity as a strategic factor for sustainable urban development; the network covers seven creative fields: Crafts and Folk Arts, Media Arts, Film, Design, Gastronomy, Music and Literature". There are 20 cities of literature around the world right now. They include: Baghdad, Melbourne, Prague, Barcelona, Iowa City, Montevideo, Kraków, Granada, Heidelberg, Dublin and, since 2015, Lviv, which has become the first Ukrainian city to join this prestigious network.

For Ukraine, which has been involved in a military conflict to safeguard its existence since 2014, being a member of this club is not only an honour but also the highest possible recognition that Ukrainian literature is a valuable asset to culture on a global scale.

A city that inspires

As a matter of fact, granting Lviv the title of UNESCO City of Literature did not come as a surprise. Those who are even a little familiar with the publishing market in Ukraine know that for Ukrainian writers, readers and publishers, New Year's Eve is not December 31st. For them, it falls on the second weekend of September, when the famous Publishers' Forum (*Forum Vydavciv*) is held in Lviv. This event not only sets the deadline for many authors and publishers but is also a date marked in the calendar of many readers. During the forum, most of the prestigious literary prizes are awarded, encapsulating a year of literary achievements.

Foreign writers who also participate in the Lviv forum often point out that unlike other large book fairs, such as those in London, Frankfurt or Leipzig, where deals are made and it is mostly about literary agents selling publishing rights while writers just smile to the cameras and sign contracts, the event in Lviv is first and foremost for the readers. In September 2015, the number of them attending the fair reached around 50,000, and I myself witnessed a situation where a Swiss poet, seeing a crowd of young people who had come to a meeting with him, said: "In my next life, I would like to be born as a Ukrainian poet."

The Lviv Publishers' Forum began in 1994. It was initiated not as the result of a decree or a governmental decision, but like the first fairs in medieval cities, where even a central square is called a market, it was a grassroots initiative that emerged from the people's needs. With the collapse of the Soviet Union, the attendant system of selling and distributing books also disappeared. Nevertheless, there remained a few publishing and printing houses that did not have contact with authors and bookshops from more remote locations, as well as bookshops that did not know where to order the latest books. This meant that all that readers could find in their local bookshops were useless communist and erotic books. There was no modern literature or new, non-ideological books. It was because of this shortage that an initiative, led by an angel of Ukrainian literature, Oleksandra Koval, was put forward, to gather everybody who was interested in books and literature in one place. The choice of location was a no brainer: the capital. However, this did not mean the capital of the state, which is Kyiv, but rather Ukraine's cultural capital, Lviv.

> The Lviv Publishers' Forum was begun in 1994 as a grassroots initiative that emerged from the people's needs.

For Ukrainians, Lviv is more than just a large metropolis in western Ukraine. Its rich and multi-cultural history, as well as its breathtaking beauty, explains why Ukraine is a part of Europe. This, in turn, explains why after Jamala's victory in the Eurovision Song Contest in May 2016 there were calls for the next contest to be organised in Lviv, not Kyiv. It is hoped that the tourists and music stars who would come to that event would be able to see how beautiful and European Ukraine really is.

This is also the reason the decision was made to organise the first book fair in independent Ukraine in Lviv. Moreover, this is why in Ukraine nobody was surprised when in December 2015 Lviv was bestowed with the title "City of Literature" and became a member of the Creative Cities UNESCO network. This recognition was just a reinforcement of something that was already obvious to many Ukrainians and Central Europeans.

Cultural centre

Even without any fancy titles, Lviv has always been a city of literature. In 1547, the first book to be published in Ukraine, titled *Apostolos* by Ivan Fedorov, was published there. Renowned writers such as Leopold von Sacher-Masoch, Simon Simonides, Ivan Franko, Stanisław Lem, Bruno Schulz, Bohdan Ihor Antonych and Adam Zagajewski lived and worked there. Even the legend of the beat generation, Allen Ginsberg, had roots here. His father came from Lviv.

Historically speaking, Lviv was an important educational and cultural centre in this part of the world. It attracted intellectuals, professors, and people of arts and literature. It was thanks to their presence that the city created so many literary clubs, bookshops and libraries. Thus, Lviv was also the city where the Ossolineum, the most important and largest collection of Polish manuscripts, books and works of art, was established in 1817. In 1947, after the post-war relocation of the Polish population to western Poland had taken place and the most valuable part of the collection had been taken to Wrocław, the site of the Ossolineum became the Stefanyk National Science Library, which today, is one of Ukraine's most important libraries.

Beyond the Stefanyk Library, Lviv is home to an additional 173 libraries. In 2013 alone, they were visited by total of 3.8 million readers, borrowing nearly ten million books. In the city there are 86 printing houses and 26 publishing houses, as well as 45 bookshops of all kinds (religious, children, etc.). By comparison, the number of bookshops in other major Ukrainian cities is usually estimated at between two and five, and almost never exceeding ten.

Lviv is also home to writers such as Yuriy Vynnychuk, Natalka Sniadanko, Maryana Savka, Viktor Neborak, Ostap Slyvynskyj, Halyna Kruk, Hryhoriy Semenchuk, Tymofiy Havryliv, Marianna Kiyanovska and others. It also hosts a very special educational institution, the Ukrainian Academy of Printing, whose most well-known graduate is the world famous Ukrainian writer Yuri Andrukhovych. Lviv University has also established one of the most influential translation schools in Ukraine. Their graduates translate from Polish, German and other Balkan languages.

In addition to the previously mentioned Publishers' Forum, which is an event targeted mainly at adults, there are also other festivities organised for readers, which include a spring fair of children's literature and a few international literary events. Together with Brno (the Czech Republic), Wrocław (Poland), Ostrava (Czech

Republic) and Košice (Slovakia), Lviv co-organises a Central European month of readings with authors. Within this framework, there are two literary meetings held every day in July. In Lviv numerous literary magazines are published and nine annual literary prizes are awarded. On top of that, there will be a new award, starting this year: the special award of the City of Literature UNESCO.

So what is this whole "city of literature" all about? We all know that there are not that many tourists in the world who would be interested in coming to a city just because it is a city of literature. "Such a prestigious title is, first of all, an effective tool," says Olha Mukha, director of the Lviv City of Literature office. "For us, it has opened a window of opportunity to make new contacts and promote the city. For both residents and tourists, it is about expanding the cultural offer. After receiving the title, the city assigned additional funding to literary activities and these are funds that we did not have in the budget before. 2.7 million hryvnias (nearly 100,000 euros) have been allocated for library projects, including interesting ideas aimed at seniors and children. In addition, almost one million hryvnias (about 36,000 euros) have been set aside to fund the operation of our office, which for all these years has officially not existed. The work that we did was carried out by the goodwill of local people and volunteers."

The people of literature

Indeed, the real miracle of Lviv being granted the title of City of Literature UNESCO is that it was achieved thanks to the work of some very enthusiastic people. They started to gather in early 2013 and organised a conference, to which they invited the city authorities, librarians, writers, journalists, NGO activists and university lecturers. Together, they prepared a proposal which was later completed by a group of specialists from different areas. They filed their application with UNESCO but were not awarded the title first time around. Despite this, instead of giving up and being disappointed, they continued to develop their programme. As the Ukrainian proverb says: "*Зі світу по нитці – бідному сорочка*", which roughly translated into English is "every little but helps". For example, someone who worked as an art manager in a café would invite everybody over for a discussion over free coffee. Librarians were providing rooms for larger strategic meetings, while others were spending their free time translating docu-

> The real miracle of Lviv being granted the title of City of Literature UNESCO is that it was achieved thanks to the work of some very enthusiastic people.

Each September Lviv hosts its annual Publisher's forum. The event in Lviv is first and foremost an event for the readers. In 2015 the number of them attending the fair reached around 50,000.

ments into English. Even the boyfriend of one of the activists was voluntarily forced to create the project's website!

Thus, when the city made its second attempt, it was finally honoured with the title. The team of volunteers received public recognition and their press conferences were suddenly being attended by politicians and government employees. The team later received an office from the city, small salaries for its staff and its first budget for literary projects. At the start of the journey, there was just an idea and a group of people who devoted their time and talents to its realisation. That is why we can say that the city of literature was built from extraordinary bricks. These bricks were Lviv's residents who are, first and foremost, the people of the city's literature.

However, people of literature can also be found beyond Lviv. They exist throughout Galicia, a region whose eastern capital was Lviv during the Habsburg Empire. The main city of western Galicia is Kraków. It is also a city whose promotional skills and successes have set an example and became an inspiration for the Lviv activists. Kraków had been making efforts to become a City of Literature UNESCO since 2010. It received this honour in 2013.

Hence, the experience and advice of colleagues in Kraków was very useful to the Lviv team. "First of all, it was our institutional and individual friends who helped us with consultations and logistics. Kraków was the first city in the Network of Creative Cities that supported our application (later, cities such as Edinburgh, Dublin, Norwich and Melbourne joined in). Now, with our colleagues in Kraków, Robert Piaskowski and Justyna Jochym, we are developing a vision for a strategic partnership. In fact, we are already undertaking joint projects: in early June, at a UNESCO meeting in Beijing, we were representing one voice of the region, and in the autumn of this year we are co-organising Kraków days in Lviv" adds Olha Mukha.

> Kraków was the first city in the Network of Creative Cities to support Lviv's efforts to become a UNESCO City of Literature.

Heritage of creativity

Worldwide, there are 20 UNESCO Cities of Literature, but the connection between Lviv and Kraków is special. It is not just the result of territorial proximity but also a shared cultural and historical heritage. The only other similar situation where two cities of literature are so close together can be found in the British Isles. Creativity is definitely a characteristic feature of Galicia. Therefore, even though it is evident that Kraków and Lviv have a lot in common, it needs to be stressed that what they share most of all is the will to develop and work together. In 2012, during preparations for the 2012 UEFA European Football Championship, which was co-hosted by Poland and Ukraine, improvements in infrastructure were undertaken which created better connections between Kraków and Lviv. Naturally, further shared improvements in the coming years will only bring Lviv closer to Poland and, more broadly, Europe. Most recently, plans were announced to build a modern, high-speed rail connection.

It is not only infrastructure that benefits from inter-city connections: the Lviv office of the City of Literature UNESCO programme, inspired by Kraków's achievements, has started a few very ambitious and popular projects. The first one that is worth mentioning is called literary mapping: creating a functional map of Lviv (both on paper and as an application for mobile devices). It will highlight important monuments and museums, as well as houses and places where different writers worked and lived. These will include not just Bohemian cafés but also, for example, places where poets had romantic encounters. The second project is creating a promotional film that presents Lviv as a city of literature, as well as the creation of a video-anthology of famous statements that different writers formulated in reference to the city. Another project, which projects the poems of contemporary writers onto the walls of various buildings (not just in the city centre but also in residential districts), has become a real hit. Unsurprisingly, selfies with poetry in the background have filled up the Instagram accounts of many young Ukrainians.

To popularise literature and reading, activists not only invite people to libraries but also reach out to them, especially in places that are frequently visited by crowds. Thus, it is becoming increasingly common to find "book food" stands at hipster street food festivals. Alternatively, activists identify remote parks where people like to spend their weekends and set up book points or book tents where you can not only borrow a book, but also enjoy reading it on the grass, in the shade while listening to good music. The activists have also reached out to the Crimean Tatars, who have left Crimea en masse following the peninsula's annexation by the Russian Federation. Many of them have migrated to Galicia. Special attention is given to projects that are addressed to people in difficult situations, especially the internally displaced who have escaped Crimea or Donbas, war veterans from eastern Ukraine, pensioners and orphans.

Such methods of popularising reading and literary culture are widely practiced in developed countries, yet for Ukraine, these are revolutionary experiences. Regardless, they have been very warmly welcomed by both residents and tourists alike. It just goes to show that the locals are right: the "L" in "Lviv" stands for "literature". NEE)

Translated by Iwona Reichardt

Andriy Lyubka is a contemporary Ukrainian poet, writer and essayist.

Literature as a legalised weapon

NATALKA SNIADANKO

There has recently been an increase both in the number of translations published in Ukraine and the number of translations of contemporary Ukrainian literature appearing abroad. Interestingly, it is Polish literature that is now the most widely recognised in Ukraine while it is also perhaps the only one holding an active dialogue with Ukrainian literature.

This all happened long ago, perhaps as much as 15 years has passed. We were sitting in the small room of a student hotel in Warsaw, putting together a collected volume of Polish essays translated into Ukrainian. The ever-restless Ola Hnatiuk was passing from one text to another, editing the translations sentence by sentence, not missing a shade of meaning, any actual or possible connotation, explaining patiently how this or that quote, metaphor or simile works according to the perception of the Polish reader and trying to find the most accurate equivalent in Ukrainian. The book was published in 2001 under the title *12 Polish essays* (*12 польських есеїв*). It was the first collection of Polish essays in Ukrainian. It would still be several years until the first translations of Polish writers like Czesław Miłosz, Zbigniew Herbert, Wisława Szymborska, as well as Olga Tokarczuk, Andrzej Stasiuk, Ziemowit Szczerek, Żanna Słoniowska, Joanna Bator, Witold Szabłowski and many others would appear in Ukrainian. At the same time, there were practically no translations of Ukrainian literature into Polish in the Warsaw bookstores, apart from a few anthologies published by enthusiasts or Yuriy Andrukhovych's *The Moscoviad*, which carried the suspicious subtitle of "a horror story".

It was still some years before the first translations into Polish of Ukrainian writers like Taras Prokhasko, Oksana Zabuzhko, Serhiy Zhadan, Mykola Riabchuk, Maria Matios, Ostap Slyvynskyi, Dzvinka Matiyash and many others would appear. Then, as now, translations appeared primarily due to the titanic efforts of enthusiasts, a good many of whom grew out of that very same seminar given by Ola Hnatiuk and Adam Pomorski. The seminar turned many of those inspired enthusiasts into skilful and experienced translators.

Envy in the east

These days, there are still more translations of Polish literature into Ukrainian than Ukrainian literature into Polish. The reason for this lies simply in the policy of the Polish Book Institute (a public institution whose aim is to promote Polish literature – editor's note) over the last fifteen years. The vast majority of translations of Polish literature into Ukrainian have been done with support from the institute, whose name is mentioned with envy in nearly every literary discussion concerning translation. This envy comes not only from Ukrainians, but also from writers of other eastern European countries whose domestic literature is promoted abroad far less professionally than that of their Polish counterparts.

> These days, there are more translations of Polish literature into Ukrainian than Ukrainian literature into Polish.

Even in comparison to many western European institutions which support translation the Polish Book Institute stands out. The German Goethe Institute, for example, which is very active in Ukraine, prioritises the translation of works by contemporary authors. Receiving a grant to translate classic works is quite difficult. Such a policy is justifiable in countries where classical literature has already been widely translated and its re-issue is considered a commercial venture. But things are different in Ukraine. There is a large number of classical texts which have yet to be translated into Ukrainian. They are known in Ukraine mainly due to their Russian translations. As a result, children are obliged to read books which appear on the school curriculum in Russian, because either there are no Ukrainian translations available or they are very difficult to find. This has negative consequences for Ukrainian culture not only because it continues the Soviet-era process of Russification but also because it makes the publication of Ukrainian translations commercially unprofitable. Thus the position of the Polish Book Institute, which continues to support translations into Ukrainian, has been especially important for Ukrainian readers. With support from the institute the works of Olga Tokarczuk

Photo courtesy of Lviv Publisher's Forum

Literature in Ukraine often plays the role of a legalised weapon, by means of which political convictions are asserted, historical myths are created and readers' tastes and affections are manipulated.

and Magdalena Tulli, as well as Zbigniew Herbert and Gustav Herling-Grudzinski, have been published.

Not only is Polish literature now the most widely recognised in Ukraine out of all world literature, it is also perhaps the only one holding an active dialogue with Ukrainian literature. We are also seeing a new trend of mutual translations. This concerns predominantly modern authors of "topical" books which have recently appeared in the original and have attracted a great deal of attention. For example, Żanna Słoniowska's book *The House with Stained Glass* and *Felix Austria* by Sofia Andrukhovych both appeared in translation – the former in Ukrainian and the latter in Polish – almost as soon as they were released in their original languages.

Against such a positive backdrop it is ever saddening to note the recent appearance in the Polish press of reports suggesting that the Polish Book Institute will change its policy regarding the promotion of literature and will now only support books of authors who are loyal to the current authorities. Meanwhile, there still does not exist any analogous structure to support translations from Ukrainian. The enthusiasm of translators to create one, therefore, should be shared by foreign publishing houses who carry all the financial risks associated with such publications.

Polish cultural institutions also take it upon themselves to promote translations from Ukrainian and into Ukrainian. This is demonstrated in particular by the international "Angelus" award, three laureates of which are Ukrainian writers. Invariably, almost all translations published from Ukrainian into Polish in any given year make it onto the list of finalists. The Joseph Conrad Korzeniowski Literary Prize, established by the Polish Institute in Kyiv and awarded to Ukrainian writers, is another example. There are also many Polish literary festivals at which Ukrainian writers are consistently among the guests. The advancement of Polish literature in Ukraine is undertaken by the Polish Institute and the Polish Book Institute. This makes it much easier to promote Polish books in Ukraine than it is to promote Ukrainian books in Poland. We can only hope the policies of the current Polish government will not affect these well-established and extremely effective channels of promotion.

***

There has recently been an increase both in the number of translations published in Ukraine and the number of translations of contemporary Ukrainian literature appearing abroad. There are even several publishing houses in Ukraine that specialise in translated literature, with translations from Polish forming the basis of their catalogue. This is particularly the case with the Lviv Publishing houses "Urbino", "Piramida" and "Astrolyabiya", the Chernivtsi Publishing House "Books XXI" and the Kyiv publishing houses "Tempora" and "Komubook". There are also publishing houses in Poland which are notable for their distinct "Ukrainian" preference, for example, "Czarne", "Biuro literackie" and "W.A.B.". The Austrian publishing house "Haymon", meanwhile, is actively translating Ukrainian writers into German.

It is also important to note which literary works Ukrainian and Polish publishers choose for translation. Interestingly, publishers from both countries are choosing literature from the "niche" segment, far from the commercial mainstream. Among the commercial projects, the historical detective novel is by far the leading genre in both countries. To be more precise, the genre began to actively develop in Ukraine soon after the appearance of the first translations of novels by Marek Krajewski. Today we see a well-established trend for Lviv detective stories, Lviv historical novels or simply novels about Lviv such as those written by Andriy Kurkov, Yuriy Vynnychuk and Bohdan Kolomiychuk, the last of whose books are already being used as the basis for filming a joint Ukrainian-Polish TV series.

The publishing market in Ukraine, as well as publishing houses around world, is suffering from a crisis caused by the elimination of paper books. Besides that, there are two more painful problems in Ukraine. The first one is competition with Russian-language books, which affects the market for translated literature more than other markets. The second problem is piracy which is not being fought at an official level. The phenomenon of new works appearing for free on pirate websites just a few weeks after being published is widespread.

When it comes to the thematic fields which interest both Ukrainian and Polish contemporary writers, there are many points of intersection. The trend for books of reportage is one example. Such works first appeared in Poland. After a few of them were translated, the genre quickly took root in Ukraine and is now developing actively. Attempts to investigate family history against a backdrop of a specific region and epoch in history are also common to literature in both countries. The Bukovinan stories of *Sweet Darusya* by Mariya Matios; the Silesian family saga of Jadzia Chmura in *Sandy Mountain* by Joanna Bator; and the Gdańsk novels *Weizer Dawidek* by Pawel Huelle or *Hanemann* by Stefan Chwin are all examples.

Aesthetics of history novels

Books on historical topics (both in translation and written by Ukrainian writers) have become popular in Ukraine in recent years. Such literature, which reinterprets the lessons of history, gained popularity in Europe long ago. Yet, the aesthetics of writing such novels both in Ukraine and abroad is quite different today than what it once was. European prose on historical topics does not seek to enlighten and is therefore often much more capable of satisfying the needs of a more demanding reader, including a Ukrainian reader. The books translated into Ukrainian by Martin Pollack, Katja Petrowskaja, Jenny Erpenbeck, Ignacy Karpowicz, Magdalena Tulli, Joanna Bator, Olga Tokarczuk and Ziemowit Szczerek, as well as the large number of works yet to be translated, offer an approach to the historical context which is rich in detail and nuance.

> In Ukraine historical novels are intended to fictionalise controversial moments of history, foster a sense of patriotism and tell a wider public about facts which were concealed during Soviet times.

In Ukraine historical novels are intended to fictionalise little-known or controversial moments of our history, foster a sense of patriotism in the reader, and tell a wider public about the facts and interpretations which were concealed during Soviet times. This mission of literature to enlighten enjoys great popularity among readers. It is badly needed given the lack of similar texts in the realms of popular science and social and political commentary. But such literature often "sins" by rendering a topic in black-and-white terms and oversimplifying facts and aesthetics. It creates overly-categorical judgements and is directed at a wide audience of undemanding readers, as opposed to focusing on solving more refined and delicate aesthetic problems. Historical themes appear either as background for another genre, for example crime or romance, or are called upon to divide historical figures into "heroes" and "traitors". This is especially true when the topic is painful and unanalysed in the society's recent history.

This is what distinguishes the Ukrainian situation from that which prevails generally in Europe. Literature here often plays the part of a legalised weapon, by means of which political convictions are asserted, historical myths are created and readers' tastes and affections are manipulated. Russian-speaking readers, on principle, read Ukrainian literature in its original and do not buy translations of it into Russian even if those translations have been published in Ukraine. The decision is, after all, more political than aesthetic. Russian-speaking writers in Ukraine often find themselves outside of the literary context, with Ukrainian publishing houses disposed, above all, to publishing contemporary Ukrainian and Ukrainian-language works.

Writers, as viewed by the ordinary reader, often become the final arbiters of morality. They can still be trusted in a world of corrupted authority, political power and media. From writers people expect not only the truth about the historical past but also truthful predictions about the future. Under such conditions, literature's function to enlighten and provide social commentary takes precedence, as its aesthetic function recedes into the background. NEE

Translated by Yulia Pelepchuk

Natalia Sniadanko is a Ukrainian writer, journalist and translator.

The writing in the (city) walls

KINGA GAJDA

Kraków is a city whose literary history is directly tied to Lviv. A literary tour through the streets of Kraków revives the stories of people and brings certain figures back to life. In this journey, one can also learn just how connected the literary history of Krakow is to Lviv.

It is never an easy task to write about cities, especially when the focus is on the past, while at the same time attempting to trace a heritage connection between the people of two particular cities. In this case, the challenge regards Kraków and Lviv. What principle should one follow to take the reader on this imaginary tour? Which of the two cities should become the main protagonist of the story? What memories should be evoked? Which fragments from the lives of which writers should be mentioned?

A tour like this usually leads from one specific building to another. It follows selected streets and takes visitors to various monuments. It takes you to places where famous people lived and shows you the streets that those people strolled. Even when all these places are not the main thread of the story, they still create a vivid picture. A story like that inevitably has to take sides: it can either focus on the buildings or the people. According to Tadeusz Boy-Żeleński, a writer and physician connected with both Kraków (where he studied and worked) and Lviv (where he settled after the outbreak of the Second World War), the walls of a city fight an eternal battle against the common people. What actually should be rescued from oblivion, he wondered, and what should be restored?

Walls and people

Boy-Żeleński notes that there are appropriate offices established to protect the walls from the people, but there is no protection of people from the walls. To illustrate the relationship between the two, he brings up an anecdote about the beginnings of the Planty Park – the pride of Kraków and one of the city's most charming and unique places. The park was born out of terrible vandalism as it was designed along the line of the old defence walls that had been completely torn down. He also mentions St Florian's Gate, and other similar gates used to stand at the end of most streets leading to the old city. They were all dismantled except for St Florian's, which escaped the same fate only because one of the city council members decided that its demolition could cause bitter winds sweeping on the main market square. Back then, Boy-Żeleński points out, intense winds on the square could "spread depravity among the believers who were on their way to church".

> Cities protect the walls from the people, but there is no protection of people from the walls.

Walls and people, as we can see, constantly interact with each other and there is a certain harmony between them. They complement and shape one another. As the poet Adam Zagajewski once wrote: "landscapes enter our soul, leaving images not only on the retina of our eye but also in the depths of our personality". Zagajewski, who was born in Lviv, was expelled along with other Poles to the city of Gliwice after the end of the Second World War. It was when he moved to Kraków to study that he first connected his professional life with the city. He worked as a lecturer at the University of Mining and Metallurgy (today the University of Science and Technology) and with the new wave poetry movement. Zagajewski tries to find the city in his poetry and narratives. He recalled that he has lost two home countries – one of them was Lviv, for which he searched in his imagination and chose poetry to guide him in this quest.

Another well-known poet and writer named Zbigniew Herbert was also born in Lviv and later studied in Kraków. In one interview he said that "The city is not a collection of buildings, monuments, squares and bridges – it is the quality of human interaction that makes up the city." One way to fill an urban space is to incorporate the stories of its people into the streets. In *Another Beauty*, the book dedicated to Kraków, Zagajewski writes: "the streets are generally absent-minded, their low foreheads do not house any ideas, despairs, or hopes. The roofs rest quietly on the old apartment buildings. Some things, however, can be easily guessed, some stories can be finished."

A heritage tour which connects artists from Kraków and Lviv can be one attempt at completing the history of the buildings with the stories of the people. In recalling his memories of Kraków, he wrote: "When I think of the past years, when I imagine that city, bring back to memory its inhabitants, passers-by filling the streets and squares, rushing somewhere or otherwise walking unhurriedly, hopping on trams at the last possible moment as they are leaving, or sitting idly on benches … when I see all that, I also see myself. I was also part of that picture." Zagajewski's story involves people and not empty streets.

Hybrid city

Kraków is a place where a large number of stories can be concentrated in a small area. The city, as Zagajewski describes it, is full of contrasts – beautiful, yet gloomy. It is permeated with cultural heritage, but also painfully marked by its history. It is a hybrid city. Boy-Żeleński, in his book dedicated to Kraków titled *Know Thou This Country?*, notes that the city, as it was shaped by various circumstances, was the most original city under the sun, and surely the most unique place of all time in the globe. Its geographical location itself is quite unique – pushed into the very corner of Galicia, having lost its status of regional capital in favour of Lviv and squashed within the walls of the Austrian fortress which did not allow for any growth. It became a small town. Yet it never abdicated from its role as the country's capital city. On the contrary, the conditions created by its subjugation preserved certain cultural values that were stifled in other regions. All this shaped Kraków into a peculiar entity. The city would later be rediscovered by the rest of the country, as it became known for its stained glass, poetry, tombs, art and lifestyle.

> Both Kraków and Lviv owed their high status to the centuries of tradition and the role that they had played in the history of the Polish nation.

Michał Rogoż recalls that during the interwar period both Kraków and Lviv were exceptionally important cities for Poland. Undoubtedly both places owed their high status to the centuries of tradition and the role that they had played in the history of the Polish nation. Both cities were home to significant and influential cultural and academic institutions in the early days of the Second Polish Republic, which after many years of subjugation was in dire need of educated people and competent experts. Between 1918 and 1939, the two cities saw some dramatic developments, yet they continued to lose their importance to Warsaw.

Kraków, however, remained the cradle of Polish culture. A heritage tour following the streets of Kraków revives the stories of people and brings back certain figures to life. And the main market square is where people come to interact. It forms a sort of theatrical space in the city. It is a meeting point for people of different cultures, religions and personal stories. As Boy-Żeleński put it: "Each dweller of Kraków would normally be at the main square around five times a day: wherever they were headed, be it a coffee shop or a bank, they had to walk across that square." For that reason, our heritage trail should be focused on the same area.

Heritage tour

Let us start our trail on Kujawska Street. It is here, in the house of the Wielow-iejski family, that Adam Ważyk (1905–1982), who lived in Lviv after the onset of the Second World War, had spent some time. In Lviv Ważyk was a member of the Union of Soviet Writers in Ukraine as well as the Patriotic Organisation of Poland. On January 22nd 1945 he participated in the first meeting of the Polish Writers' Union on Kujawska Street. The main issue on the agenda was establishing a daily newspaper in Kraków, called the *Kraków Daily*. As Witold Zechenter recalls: "on January 25th, early in the morning, a loud banging on my flat's door woke me up. [Stanisław] Balicki shouted at me: 'Get up, we're going to Wielopole (a street in Kraków), we're making a newspaper!' In less than an hour I was on site ready to start my new post-war job. I joined three other people and together we set up the first post-occupation daily in Kraków – the *Kraków Daily* ... the other three were Jacek Fruehling (editor-in-chief), Balicki (responsible for the equipment) and Adam Ważyk."
This is how the newspaper, in which top writers would later contribute, came into existence. Until 2011 the *Kraków Daily* was headquartered in the building on the corner of Wielopole and Starowiślna Streets in Kraków. Many writers connected with Lviv also collaborated with the publication (later renamed the *Polish Daily*). One of them was Aleksander Baumgardten (1908–1980) – a Polish poet and prose writer born in Kraków who lived and worked in Lviv until 1944. In Lviv, he was a founding member of the Polish Academic Corporation Cresovia Leopoliensis. Józef Bieniasz (1892–1961), a prose writer and playwright, who studied in Lviv and worked there as a journalist, settled in Kraków after the Second World War. There was also Wilam Horzyca (1889–1959), a writer born in Lviv and theatre director who was head of the municipal theatre and the Grand Theatre in Lviv. Horzyca also directed plays at the Słowacki Theatre in Kraków.
Continuing our tour, we head towards Mickiewicz Avenue, where the Jagiellon-ian Library has been located since 1940. First, we should stop at the street named

after Leopold Staff (1878–1957) a poet born in Lviv. While studying in Lviv, he was an editor of the academic paper called *Youth* that for a short while was published in Kraków on Sławkowska Street. The motif of the city and the metaphor of wandering to a mysterious, non-existing, imaginary city, that became a part of the writer's quest for self is repeatedly found in Staff's works. This symbolic wandering is reminiscent of the real-life wanderings that were a part of Staff's life experience. In each of the places he visited, he would leave behind a bit of himself, and at the same time, taking a portion of the city away with him.

The next stop on our trail is the Jagiellonian Library, which Zagajewski and his friends would call "the botanical garden of ideas". This place was very special to him. It is here where Leszek Elektorowicz, a poet and prose writer born in 1924, worked between 1950 and 1956. Elektorowicz, born in Lviv, studied at the Jagiellonian University and collaborated with literary publications as well the Nowodworski High School in Kraków. He was on the editing team of the weekly magazine *Literary Decade* that was published on Wielopole Street. Among other writers collaborating with this weekly was Stanisław Lem (1921–2006) whose family had been repatriated to Kraków from Lviv where he had been born. Elektorowicz was also a close childhood friend of Zbigniew Herbert.

Heading towards the Jagiellonian Univeristy, where Herbert studied, it is worth stopping for a moment on Mała Street. At house number 5 is where Mariana Eile (1945–1969), born in Lviv, had lived. In 1945 Eile founded the cultural-literary magazine *Cross Section* which had considerable influence on Polish journalism. Although published in Kraków, the magazine was also well-known to readers in Lviv – indeed the city itself would often become a topic of discussion on its pages. Eile remained the chief editor for 24 years. Until 2002 the magazine's editorial office was located in Kraków; it then moved to Warsaw for a short period, before again returning to Kraków, on Ślusarska Street.

***

At our next stop – in the Collegium Novum building of the Jagiellonian University – we once again follow in the footsteps of Zbigniew Herbert. In his poetry, he would often invoke the cultural heritage of Lviv, presenting it as part of European culture. According to Jerzy S. Osowski, a Polish professor of literature, Herbert presented a socio-cultural diagnosis of the interwar generation of intelligentsia in Lviv. In his poem "My Father", Herbert wrote about his youth spent in Lviv and describes the intelligentsia inhabiting the city. He claimed that a requisite for any culture to exist is its continuity. This continuity pertains also to European culture and its disruption would result in the decay of European art. That is why Herbert described reality from the point of view of someone from Kraków, from Lviv, and later from Warsaw, but above all he described it as a European. In his literary works, he attempted to create a dialogue between men and their everyday life, he also searched for the answers to some universal questions and believed that culture involves education aimed at higher values.

The next stop is the Collegium Maius building which through 1940 housed the university library. It was here that Żegota Pauli (1814–1895) an editor, publisher, translator and historiographer of the Jagiellonian University worked. Żegota was greatly involved in the literary and political life of Lviv. As a librarian, he focused on preserving national treasures and edited source documents. He worked on the publication of works by Jan Długosz (a 15th century historian). He lived in the Palace under the Rams on the Main Market Square. There's an epitaph to his memory at St Anne's Church and a commemorative plaque dedicated to him on the wall of the monastery of the Boni Fratres order on Krakowska Street. Next to the former library building, on Jagiellońska Street, was the editorial office of *New Reform*, a daily published from 1882 to 1923. Its editor in chief was Tadeusz Romanowicz (1843–1904), born in Lviv, a member of the Galicia parliament, a writer and member of the Lviv branch of the Polish Gymnastic Society "Sokół". Among the writers who contributed to *New Reform* was Karol Irzykowski who attended school and university in Lviv and later worked there as a stenographer and reporter. In Lviv, he also collaborated with local newspapers, and after moving to Kraków in 1908, he began working for the government press agency. Irzykowski considered literary criticism, which was his domain, to be on par with literature.

After that, we stop at Szczepański Square. This place is connected with the renowned painter and playwright Bronisława Rychter-Janowska (1868–1953). She made her debut as a painter in 1896 and was closely connected with the Kraków Society of Friends of the Arts, which was initially headquartered in the Larisch Palace on the corner of Szczepański Square and Bracka Street, and later moved to Szczepański Square in 1901. The same year several of her paintings were exhibited in the newly erected palace, among them a piece titled "Wreaths". She was a frequent guest at the municipal theatre located on the Holy Ghost Square. Rychter-Janowska was also connected with the literary cabaret "Green Balloon" that performed at the Lviv coffee shop owned by Apolinary Michalik and located on Floriańska Street. Rychter-Janowska first lived in the Dębniki district and later moved to Dunajewski Street. It was in Lviv, however, that she married Tadeusz Rychter and became

> In his literary works, Zbigniew Herbert attempted to create a dialogue between men and their everyday life.

actively involved with the newly established Polish Artist Union and collaborated with the Lviv branch of the Friends of the Arts Society.

Non-linear stories

Barely passing through the old town's market square, we turn onto St John's Street – one of the favourite walking places of Stanisław Lem. The writer described his childhood spent in Lviv in his autobiographical novel *Highcastle: A Remembrance*. He often compared both cities when interviewed, once noting "opposite from our house there was the Ewers lending library, quite similar to the one in Kraków on St John's Street". He probably meant the lending library run by a well-known antiquarian book-seller and editor named Stefan Kamiński – located on St John's Street. Similarly, Zagajewski also looked for places reminiscent of Lviv when wandering the streets of Kraków. His favourite was the walking trail heading towards the Kościuszko mound. He would also take frequent strolls down Floriańska Street, Długa Street and sometimes he wandered around the main square – to describe it all later in his books.

It is time to walk across the main market square – a place frequently referred to in the work of Juliusz Kaden-Bandrowski. He would write about the great "monster" statues adorning the cloth hall (he lived across from it), the stairs leading to the back door of the Town Hall that were guarded by a stone lion, and the lilacs blooming in the Planty Park where he and his mother would stroll when going to his grandmother's for cookies. On their way, Kaden-Bandrowski and his grandmother would stop for a glass of soda water with syrup for two cents.

We finally reach Bracka Street – the place closely connected with the life of Maria Stobecka (1912–1978), a poet from Lviv. She worked as a librarian at the public library located on Bracka Street between 1945 and 1975. There she would also give talks to young people, organise story telling events and fairy-tale evenings for children. Starting in 1945 the library was located in the Palace under the Rams and functioned as the public library of the city. When the regional public library was opened on that site in 1949, the city library was moved to the Larisch Palace on Bracka Street. In 1955 the city and regional libraries merged and existed as a single library, only to become separated again after three years apart. Ending with Stobecka's footsteps, we reach Krasińkiego Street and the home of the Polish music publishing house where she sometimes found herself writing ballads to Sibellius' music.

This nearly two-hour walk through Kraków, following the stories of writers connected with both Kraków and Lviv, is only one out of many possibilities. Creating yet another urban reality, it allows literature to broaden its sphere of influence. As Nathaniel D. Wood, an American historian, writes in his essay "The 'Polish Mecca', the 'Little Vienna on the Vistula' or 'Big-City Cracow'? Imagining Cracow before the Great War": "Vienna is known for its musicians, Munich for its painters, Warsaw for its actors and Cracow for its writers".

The city walls in Kraków have a lot to tell. They hide their own stories which are often non-linear, deeply rooted in the urban tissue and must be discovered by everyone individually. Those unmarked, invisible trails unravelling as one reads the works or biographies of the writers liven up the history of the city. NEE

> Following the stories of writers connected with both Kraków and Lviv allows literature to broaden its sphere of influence.

Translated by Agnieszka Rubka

Kinga Gajda is an assistant professor at the institute of European Studies of the Jagiellonian University in Kraków. She holds a PhD in literature.

The cradle of literary Poland

An interview with Robert Piaskowski,
deputy director for programming at the Kraków
Festival Office. Interviewer: Iwona Reichardt

IWONA REICHARDT: In 2014 Kraków was named a UNESCO City of Literature. What does this title mean for the city and what does it require?

ROBERT PIASKOWSKI: Kraków was the first Slavic and second non-English speaking city in the Creative Cities UNESCO network. It was an important sign of expanding the creative cities programme into continental Europe, as earlier this title was granted to such cities as (or cities such as) Edinburgh, Iowa City, Melbourne, Dublin, Norwich and Reykjavik. With the exception of the latter, the English language dominated. The programme, however, was created to promote the idea of creativity and cities' sustainable development centred on a selected field: literature, music, new media, culinary arts, folk art, artisanship, film or performing arts. I had the pleasure of participating from the very beginning in our city's decision-making as to which area we would choose in our application form. The application's preparation involved enormous efforts with a very large group of experts: university professors, writers, translators, librarians, cultural managers, representatives of Kraków's leading and most distinguished publishers and NGO activists.

It was a long process, one that lasted for nearly four years. At that time it seemed that Kraków was already an unquestionable literary capital and thus we expected "a red carpet" reception into the network. Yet, our application overlapped with a deep crisis within the UNESCO programme which resulted in its suspension for nearly two years. And yet, it was these expectations and hopes that were vital for the importance of receiving this title. It was also the arduous unification of various groups that caused a really empowering experience and real change. Many of these groups had not worked together before and were even competing for resources, visibility, audience and media attention. The title City of Literature became a link, a beautiful altruistic idea which released a new sense and allowed for a greater integrated development of the city's identity.

How did you decide on literature for the application? As Poland's cultural capital, there are many creative fields to choose from.

At first it was difficult to decide which area to focus on for the creative cities application. We had wonderful music festivals in Poland, many wonderful composers, including Krzysztof Penderecki, and the status of Kraków orchestras were a strong mandate to obtain the title in this area. Films are also one of Kraków's strengths, with various festivals, traditions and attractive locations. We chose literature, however, since we believed it was the best expression of our city's identity. Kraków is the cradle of literary Poland, the location of Poland's first printing house and scriptoria. It is here at the Kraków Market Square where the oldest European bookshop can be found. The city has libraries which have survived the tragedy of war. Kraków is the only city in history where two recipients of the Nobel Prize in Literature lived at the same time – Wisława Szymborska and Czesław Miłosz. It is the city where Józef Konrad Korzeniowski (Joseph Conrad) studied and where Stanisław Lem created his most important works. It is here where the publishing market is con-

centrated and excellent translators live and work. The city lives by literature and literary festivals attract crowds of readers.

However, it is important to note that the title "City of Literature" is not a trophy or a sign of recognition for a glorious past. First and foremost it is an obligation for the development of the entire literary sector. I use this term, which seems unfit for literature, on purpose. We are still talking about literature not only through the prism of values, history and stories but also through the prism of the book market and the whole profession. Today's Kraków is a city of an extraordinary concentration of creative entrepreneurship related to literature. Around 30 per cent of people who are employed in the creative sector in our region work in this literary sector.

Kraków received the title City of Literature thanks to the work of many generations of artists who lived and worked here. Their fates, however, differed. Not all of them could work and write in favourable conditions, and yet they produced great works. What is the city's literary life like today? Can we assume that Kraków will continue to give the world great writers and poets?

In March 2015 our city announced a programme to support literary debuts. This included the Conrad Award for the best debut in the category of "prose" and a very popular City of Literature UNESCO course on creative writing. Last year, together with the Polish Book Institute and the *Tygodnik Powszechny*

Foundation, we implemented a grant programme called "Promotors of Debuts" which is aimed at publishers who are investing in new writers. The reason for this is based on our analysis of the situation in the Polish publishing market. We came to the conclusion that fewer refreshing names and voices have appeared in recent years. During the 20th century Polish literature generated an impressive number of brilliant writers in practically all areas: poetry, theatre, reportage, etc. Therefore, it is crucial we provide the new generation with the right conditions, but more than anything help rebuild the social prestige of literature as an area of art in which our identity is created and expressed. This is an enormous task indeed and it is difficult to assess from today's perspective, especially considering that readership rates continue to decrease in Poland.

However, the success of Kraków's literary festivals and the growing number of visitors to the annual International Book Fair provides hope that the future is not so dim. In addition, there is a clear revival of artistic books, there are more and more new niche publishers and self-publishing is becoming increasingly popular. In districts outside the city centre, thematic bookshops are being opened which serve as local cultural centres. New thematic micro-festivals are created focusing on crime novels, comic books, reportage, etc. This diversity is indeed very great. We recently counted that in the last year alone we organised or supported almost 300 separate literary events with a total participation of 130,000 readers. These are impressive statistics.

Since 2011 Kraków is also a member of the International Cities of Refuge Network (ICORN), an organisation that offers help to writers and artists who cannot work in their own cities or states. What activities does the city undertake to help writers who are discriminated in their homelands? Is it ad hoc assistance or has the city managed to develop long-term contacts, both with artists and between them?

Kraków was selected by the ICORN leadership as a city whose history and geographic location have directly determined its presence in the network. This was largely thanks to Salman Rushdie's inspiration. Rushdie, who experienced the threat of fatwa and home imprisonment, knew that in the world of global political conflict only cities can offer shelter to persecuted writers. The rule is simple. A city offers hospitality for a period of one or two years to a writer whose life is in danger in his/her homeland as a result of his/her writing. Since 2011 Kraków has hosted six writers from Russia, Egypt, Iran, Belarus, Turkey and the Democratic Republic of Congo. Kraków turned out to be a place of asylum and a creative bay; it was during his stay in Kraków that Lawon Barszczeuski translated Stanisław Przybyszewski's *Śnieg* into Belarusian and where Aslı Erdoğan was named one of the 50 most promising writers in the world by the French magazine *Lire*. The

Photo: Adam Golec / Kraków Festival Office

presence of each stipend recipient within the ICORN programme has become an opportunity to bring attention to the deep and organic relations between literature and human rights, especially freedom of speech.

Both within the ICORN and UNESCO networks, Kraków can also be seen as a "window to the East". What activities undertaken by the city allow us to say that such a statement is a fact and not just a vague notion?
Recently we held the fifth edition of the Czesław Miłosz Festival, today the largest poetic event in Poland, which is a continuation of the tradition of the famous Meetings of Poets from the East and the West initiated by Czesław Miłosz

and Wisława Szymborska in 1997. The main theme of this year's edition was Miłosz's *Roadside Dog*. We invited guests to reflect on the topics of refugees and spiritual wanderers which are so important in times of unprecedented flows of people and cultures, such as those which we are seeing today. Last year during the Conrad Festival's sixth edition, we had the honour of hosting Svetlana Alexievich right after she was awarded the Nobel Prize in Literature. The experiences that these wonderful poets and writers share fit into the long tradition of Kraków as a city of shelter and literary freedom.

In the autumn of 2015 the city of Lviv in Ukraine also received the title UNESCO City of Literature. Lviv and Kraków share many connections, which now includes this title. Have there been any activities undertaken together, or are such plans being made?

In fact, we started our applications for the title at the same time. I remember in 2011 when Hryhoriy Semenchuk, a young poet, literary activist and musician, came to Kraków. At that time we met with representatives from Edinburgh, Madrid, Iowa City, Melbourne and Dublin as well as from Ljubljana and Napoli; in other words, the cities which already had the title and those that were interested in applying. This meeting gave impetus not only to us but also to representatives from Lviv. Later, I visited Lviv during the Publishers' Forum and presented the city our ideas. I was greatly impressed by the large number of people who came out to hear my presentation. Kraków has been very supportive of Lviv's application for the city of literature. Lviv and Kraków are cities with a shared history and many years

of partnership. We were thrilled when we learned that after three years of hard work, Lviv was also named a City of Literature,, thus moving our partnership into new directions.

All I can say at this point is to expect much more to come from our partnership. We are already planning celebrations commemorating the 100th birthday of Stanisław Lem, who also has connections to Lviv, and we will be visiting Lviv during the Festival of Good Neighbourhood. In October we will be initiating a project anchoring ICORN in the Baltic Sea Region, which will connect institutions from Kraków, Lviv and the Swedish city of Växjö. For this occasion we are planning on publishing a cookbook with literary texts describing our culinary traditions, as well as organising programmes of discussions and lectures in reference to the International Day of the Imprisoned Writer on November 15th. And Lviv will be an honorary guest next year at the Miłosz Festival. (NEE)

Translated by Iwona Reichardt

Robert Piaskowski is the deputy director for programming at the Kraków Festival Office.

Iwona Reichardt is the deputy editor in chief of *New Eastern Europe*.

Books are life

An interview with Oleksandra Koval, founder
and head of the Lviv Publishers' Forum.
Interviewer: Olesya Yaremchuk

OLESYA YAREMCHUK: In 2015 Lviv received the status as a "UNESCO City of Literature". What does this title mean for you and the city?

OLEKSANDRA KOVAL: Lviv is a city which has something to share with the world: its great history of literature, which dates back to the times of Ivan Fedorov and continues through to the Ruska Trinity, Ivan Franko, Sholem Aleichem, Stanisław Lem and many others. Where else can one come across such diversity? Lviv has an active literary life. There is the 23-year-old tradition of the Lviv Publisher's Forum which changed this city. New festivals keep appearing like the "Month of Authors' Readings" and plenty of smaller literary events are held. There are numerous bookstores and libraries with valuable catalogues and a number of language departments at the universities which prepare future literary critics and writers. The status of "UNESCO City of Literature" seems to be well-deserved.

It seems also to be a good excuse to tell the world about us. The great histor-ical figure Ivan Franko, for example, is too little-known outside Ukraine. And by organising readings of Stanisław Lem, we can also shift interest for his person-ality and creative works towards the city where he was born. After all, apart from anything else this status can also attract tourists and will allow us to add "liter-ary" tourists to the great number of the already existing ones.

Lviv received the title of "UNESCO City of Literature" owing to the literary work of generations of writers. What is literary life like today in Lviv? How do you see it in the future?

The situation today is much better when compared to what it was like even ten or 15 years ago. At that time the main problem was a lack of attention towards culture in the media. Frankly speaking, the Ukrainian mass media did much to degrade our people's cultural awareness. We still need a great deal more time to overcome this trauma. But of course I do not give up hope that our literary life will recover and become livelier. People from other cities say we have nothing to complain about but I am convinced we can do better. The focus of our attention should be on the revitalisation of the libraries. I would really like them to be turned from the depositories that they are now to free open spaces, filled with books, interesting people and ideas. A no less important direction is the promotion of reading for children in families and schools. This is what the city authorities and the community should concentrate on.

Why are books so valuable for me? And why do I do all these things? Books are life. I would like to see more bookshelves appear in cafés and I would like libraries to become meeting places for children to understand what reading is while they are still in school. A few years ago during the Lviv Publishers' Forum we were visiting schools, organising meetings with pupils and talking about writers. For most of the pupils (and even the teachers) the novelty was the fact that the writer was someone alive, often young and handsome, who walked the same streets and lived nearby. They were still thinking that a writer was only a book on the shelf or a portrait on the wall.

It is also important to remember that the "UNESCO City of Literature" is not a project having a beginning and an end. This status remains valid as long as the city meets the high requirements. If we want to stay the course we will have to change our lifestyle and make every Lviv resident understand that he or she is living in a city of literature and to make every tourist feel it in the cobblestones.

Many European countries, including Ukraine, are currently facing certain challenges such as socio-political shifts, revolution or even war. What in your opinion is the role of literature in times of these transformations? How is cultural life formed under such conditions?

When you are watching relaxed tourists taking a stroll and seeing their peaceful, smiling faces in this consumer's paradise it seems that there is no war. But this is only for show. The owners of the café we are sitting in are constantly helping our army, transporting necessary items to the "Anti-Terrorist Operation" zone. Lots of families have had one of their members injured or killed and no one knows whose home will be disturbed by sad news next. Yet, it is impossible to live long in a state of tension, fear and diffidence. Our psyche forces our stress out and demands we compose ourselves, it demands we reduce our adrenaline level. This is how a certain detachment from reality appears and makes us create a semblance of a calm and peaceful life.

There is an element of culture which is a reflection – a reinterpretation of war and a military situation in our minds, but there is also another element, which abstracts. I believe there are a great many attempts today to create literature in the context of war or to talk about war in the context of literature. Probably too little time has passed for us to comprehend this war to fully process it. If we want our literary works to be read in 20, 50 or 100 years – we have to take a step back. If we are disputing whether culture

Photo: Olesya Yaremchuk

has the right to exist during wartime or whether muses should stay silent when the cannons roar, history gives us the answer to that question. Culture allows us to tear ourselves away from the urgent problems. Culture heals, strengthens and gives hope.

Lviv is sometimes referred to as a "window to the West". Which activities in the field of literature, in your opinion, allow you to affirm this?

It seems to me that geographical position is not much of a determinant in our globalised world. However, the fact that Lviv is so close to the western border and has a big airport does have significance. It is through Lviv which we can reveal our literature to the world. But there is so much work to do if we want to achieve this. A good place to start is to create residencies for translators into Ukrainian as well as for authors and literary critics from all over the world. We need to organise conferences on literary criticism and organise classes and workshops for all specialists in the spheres of publishing, reading and literature. We need to develop existing festivals which includes building new venues for big events.

The translation of literature is one of the most essential things which must be done. The translation of world literature into Ukrainian (nowadays Russian translations predominate, although this is changing) and vice versa. We need to look for and prepare new editors, translators and managers of culture, all of whom will be able to produce a high-quality Ukrainian product.

As for East-West relations, I remember Poland during the time of Leszek Balcerowicz's economic reforms. It was tough, but in just a few years great strides were made. When we had just become independent, Poland and Ukraine were practically on the same level even in the book publishing sphere. But by 1995 a gap was visible. Instead of uniting the whole nation (or at least the representatives of the book publishing sphere) and overcoming the difficult times together, everybody began to focus on their own survival at the expense of others. The state crossed culture off of the list of interests.

In the Soviet Union there was an ideology and propaganda, therefore book publishing and film production were supported and were constantly developing. In independent Ukraine they seemed to give up on explicit propaganda and so culture, which in the minds of our "leaders" only serves ideology, has become useless. Money allocated to maintain the networks of cultural institutions stagnated and there were no investment in development. Adherents of conspiracy theories believe that the neglect of the needs of the cultural sphere by the government was a devious plan to leave Ukraine under the cultural, that is to say ideological, influence of Russia. In light of recent events, it is hard not to disagree with this assertion. ᴺᴱᴱ

Translated by Yulia Pelepchuk

Oleksandra Koval is the founder and president of the Ukrainian Publishers' Forum, an annual event International Literary Festival held each September since 1994.

Olesya Yaremchuk is a freelance journalist based in Lviv.

New analysis on the Visegrad States' Reactions to the Russia-Ukraine conflict

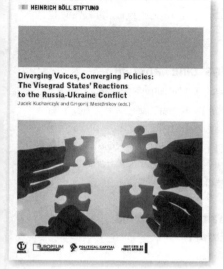

HEINRICH BÖLL STIFTUNG

**Diverging Voices, Converging Policies:
The Visegrad States' Reactions
to the Russia-Ukraine Conflict**
Jacek Kucharczyk and Grigorij Mesežnikov (eds.)

EUROPEUM   POLITICAL CAPITAL   INSTITUTE OF PUBLIC AFFAIRS

The latest publication commissioned by the Heinrich Böll Foundation in Prague and Warsaw aims to explain the differing reactions of individual Visegrad countries to the Russia-Ukraine conflict, as well as to analyse the role of the V4 Group in the EU.

Particular consideration was given to the complex historical experiences, public opinions, economic relations, as well as energy and foreign policy of Poland, Hungary, Slovakia, and the Czech Republic.

Co-publishers: Europeum – Institute for European Policy (Czech Republic), Institute of Public Affairs (Poland), Institute for Public Affairs (Slovakia), Political Capital Policy Research & Consulting Institute (Hungary)

The report can be downloaded from
https://pl.boell.org/en/publications.

HEINRICH BÖLL STIFTUNG
WARSZAWA

The Heinrich Böll Foundation is a catalyst for green visions and policy reforms and an international network working in over **60** countries in the spheres of civic education, cross-cultural dialogue, peacebuilding, and ecology. It stands for social emancipation and self-determination, as well as respect for minorities. Its projects promote dialogue between society, NGOs, politics, academia, and business.

Common European values, gender democracy and sustainability are both central tenets and cross-cutting themes for the **Warsaw Office**, which conducts three programmes – **International Politics, Democracy & Human Right**s and **Energy & Climate**.

Follow its activities on the Polish-English website **www.pl.boell.org**, Facebook, Twitter and YouTube.

The dialogue continues online...

www.neweasterneurope.eu

While you wait for your next issue of *New Eastern Europe* stay connected with the latest opinions and analysis from Central and Eastern Europe at our website which is updated regularly with exclusive content. Here are some of the articles that have been most popular recently.

A Real House of Cards: Trump, Putin and Yanukovych

Taras Kuzio,
Canadian Institute of Ukrainian Studies

Both candidates in this year's US presidential election have accepted donations from Ukrainian oligarchs and Ukraine's former president, Viktor Yanukovych.

It's a "boys' club" after all

Iwona Reichardt, New Eastern Europe

Despite the fact that there are a number of female specialists in the area of Eastern European politics and post-Soviet space in Poland, conference organisers tend to promote all-male panels.

Kaliningrad – the troubled man of Europe

Sergey Sukhankin

Amidst tumultuous 1990s many predicted that Kaliningrad would soon become either a "Baltic Hong Kong" or the "Fourth Baltic Republic." The past 25 years have instead led to a great disappointment.

Real and imagined problems of the Roma community in Slovakia

An Interview with Alexander Mušinka – co-author of "Strategy of the Slovak Republic for Integration of Roma up to 2020".

 Follow us on Twitter > @NewEastEurope

 Join us on Facebook > www.facebook.com/NewEasternEurope

 Sign up for our weekly newsletter > http://neweasterneurope.eu/newsletter